T0304337

MANUEL MAPLES ARCE

STRIDENTIST POEMS

*Translated from Spanish
and with an introduction by
KM Cascia*

WORLD POETRY

First Edition, First Printing, 2023
ISBN 978-1-954218-11-6

World Poetry Books
New York, NY
www.worldpoetrybooks.com

Distributed in the US by SPD/Small Press Distribution
www.spdbooks.org

Distributed in the UK by Turnaround Publisher Services
www.turnaround-uk.com

Library of Congress Control Number: 2022948957

Cover design by Andrew Bourne
Typesetting by Don't Look Now
Printed in Lithuania by KOPA

World Poetry Books is committed to publishing exceptional translations
of poetry from a broad range of languages and traditions, bringing the
work of modern masters, emerging voices, and pioneering innovators
from around the world to English-language readers in affordable trade
editions. Founded in 2017, World Poetry Books is a 501(c)(3) nonprofit
and charitable organization based in New York City and affiliated with
the Humanities Institute and the Translation Program at the University
of Connecticut (Storrs).

Table of Contents

Introduction:
On Maples Arce and Stridentism

In 1976, when he was twenty-three, Roberto Bolaño made one of his few attempts to play nice with the literary establishment in Mexico. It was then fifty years since the heyday of the country's major modernist avant-garde movement, *Estridentismo* (Stridentism), and the usual anniversary retrospectives were under way. Academic studies were published, gallery exhibits were hung, and there was a market for articles on the subject. So Bolaño wrote one, though it is not clear whether he was freelancing, or did so on assignment. The article, consisting of interviews with three of Stridentism's central figures, appeared that November, in the magazine *Plural*, under the amusingly literal title "Three Stridentists in 1976."

Two of the interviews, with prose writer Arqueles Vela and poet Germán List Arzubide, went as expected. Both men were eager to talk, and Bolaño knew the material well. He brought a few friends and a tape recorder, everyone had a lively chat, and he left with the recording. But when the time came to interview Stridentism's founder, Manuel Maples Arce, things didn't go as smoothly. A version of what happened is narrated in Bolaño's roman à clef on the period, *The Savage Detectives (Los detectives salvajes)*. Though that work is somewhat dubious as a historical source—entirely accurate in one place, warped by self-mythologizing in another—most of the details about this specific incident are confirmed by the *Plural* article.

Maples was then seventy-six, about ten years retired from a long career in the diplomatic corps. He received Bolaño and his friends in his apparently large and luxurious home, where Turkish coffee was served in a room full of Maples's vast library and art collection. But when the tape recorder came out, Maples refused to let them turn it on. In the novel, Bolaño has Maples say that he dislikes tape recorders "for the same reason my friend Borges dislikes mirrors." Whether or not any such name dropping actually happened, it's clear that the older poet was lording it over the younger poets. Maples insisted that Bolaño write all his questions down, which he did, leaving the questionnaire behind and returning a few days later to pick it up.

In the article, Bolaño writes that they spent most of their time with Maples "listening to him tell beautiful anecdotes," and goes on to note something that struck him as curious: "Paradoxically, the founder of Stridentism seems to be the one who grants it the least importance." There were reasons for this—reasons that Bolaño, having interviewed the other two Stridentists, must have known in 1976. Reasons that inform the use made of Stridentism in his 1998 novel, and that had everything to do with how Stridentism had unfolded in the 1920s.

As Bolaño learned firsthand, anything Maples Arce said about Stridentism has to be checked against the historical record, with special attention paid to when it was said. Statements made while the movement was active have a marked, often hilarious tendency toward exaggeration, glamorization, and myth making. Things said after the movement collapsed tend to either downplay Stridentism, both as a historical movement and a part of Maples's literary career, or erase it altogether. But on the rare occasions when Stridentism could be neither denied nor minimized, Maples never lost his habit of claiming the entire thing was entirely his own idea and doing, in accordance with a plan he had had all along. These are in keeping with many similarly revisionist artistic legends, such as those told by George Lucas about his space operas. As with Lucas, however, so with Maples: the textual history of the work flatly contradicts such claims; other people had very important roles indeed, and the truth is much more interesting than the legend.

Stridentism was remarkable for its agitprop-style fabulism, even among the archfabulists of the historical avant-gardes. The question of the movement's origin is an excellent example, existing as it does in various versions. The most common, embellished version holds that, in December of 1921, Maples Arce, alone, concluded that the time had long since come for Mexican literature to enter the 20th century, much as the country itself was doing following its long, messy revolution. So, as one did in those days, he wrote a manifesto. To this he appended an "Avant-Garde Directory." Gesturing at the form of a phonebook, this was a list of some two hundred names, all of writers and artists working along similar lines to those advocated in the manifesto. Something reasonably close to every such artist of any importance in the entire world was on the list. The text completed, Maples then went to a nearby orphanage (!) that operated a printer's workshop. There, he had the orphans run off a huge number of copies, in the form of a broadsheet. Maples then spent the night, alone, wheat pasting these posters up all over Mexico City. The next day, Mexico awoke to Maples's provocation. The old guard was scandalized, the young flocked to his banner, and Stridentism was born. Cute story. Mostly false.

The more accurate version, while perhaps less exciting, makes a lot more sense. Maples certainly wrote the manifesto alone, perhaps in a single evening, though probably not. But it was not the first Stridentist text he published. That distinction must be reserved for Maples's poem "Those Electric Roses..." which appeared four months before the manifesto, in issue 33 (September, 1921) of the Spanish literary magazine *Cosmópolis*, an organ of the Ultraist movement, whose most famous member was Jorge Luis Borges. Maples actually cites this poem in the manifesto, as an example of Stridentist poetics. But because that poem had been published in a very little magazine in Spain, very few people in Mexico had seen it. The bit about the orphanage might be true, though it is an improbably picturesque detail. Both the number of copies printed and the area of the city where they were posted simply must be exaggerated. The effect that the legendary version of events ascribes to the manifesto's appearance is pure fiction. This is not to say that the manifesto had no effect, so much as that Maples's fables had a tendency to conflate the movement with the manifesto, and to radically shrink the time scale involved, from the year plus it took for the movement to coalesce to a single week or thereabouts following the manifesto's publication.

Whatever its relation to the movement's origin, the manifesto is one of the most interesting texts of its kind. It is as bombastic as could ever be wished, a hurtling mass of text flung in the face of a literary old guard that was perhaps more vulnerable to such a critique than any other in the world. It's also a better guide to the aesthetics of its movement than most manifestos. Stridentism has long been dismissed as a mere import of the aesthetics of the European avant-garde, especially Italian Futurism. A close study of the two tendencies, however, reveals important differences, both aesthetic and, especially, political. The more direct influences on Stridentism were clearly Ultraism and Creationism, the movement founded by Chilean poet Vicente Huidobro.

The basic tenets of Stridentism stated in the manifesto share much with those of these two groups: 1) dispensing with extraneous elements derived from cinema or art, so as to focus on a deepening of the poetic image and 2) an emphasis on emotional realities rooted in the material, i.e. modern, world. The appended "Directory" clearly demonstrates that Maples's knowledge of the avant-garde was literally encyclopedic. Such a thorough list would be difficult to put together today, even with the internet at one's disposal. To do so in 1921 was truly remarkable, and speaks to the fact that Maples was drawing on ideas from avant-garde artists and writers all over the world, many of whom he was in direct contact with. His project was not to copy or impersonate them, but rather to synthesize their methods and adapt them to Mexico. As a statement of aesthetic principles resulting from this process, the manifesto served its purpose. It served another purpose too, in which the legend played a key role.

The following summer, in 1922, Maples published *Inner Scaffolds*. While this was Maples's second volume of poetry, the first dated from before his aesthetic radicalization, making *Inner Scaffolds* the first Stridentist book. The manifesto itself and its surrounding publicity were essentially a viral marketing campaign for the book. The manifesto was sincere: both the intensity of the text and the subsequent use of its ideas in Maples's poems prove that. Still, even by 1921, this kind of antic self-promotion was very common amongst avant-garde groups. From Marinetti's cars to Oliverio Girondo parading around Buenos Aires with a scarecrow when his book *Scarecrow* came out, to the Dada cabaret shows and beyond, this kind of thing was always part of the show. In Maples's case, as in the others, it was about drawing attention to the work and drawing like-minded people toward him. It worked, though not nearly as fast as Maples would later claim. And it took a bit more than one manifesto to do it.

For one thing, the 1921 manifesto was not the only such text Stridentism produced. There were somewhere between three and six of them, depending on what precisely constitutes a manifesto and who, among the group, accepted a given text. Nor was the 1921 text a standalone document, but rather the first issue of a periodical called *Actual* (Now), which ran for three issues. *Actual* gave way to another, much more ambitious periodical, called

Irradiador (Radiator), edited by the avant-garde artist Fermín Revueltas, which—though it also lasted only three issues, spanning the autumn of 1923—stands as one of the major publications of the Latin American avant-garde.

But it was arguably *Inner Scaffolds* itself that did the most to advance and grow Stridentism. The book's publication was very much one of those enormous scandals of avant-garde history which seem barely comprehensible a century later. Arqueles Vela told Bolaño that "most of the critics in those days . . . attacked the spirit of the book," as well as "Maples Arce personally." One critic had nothing to say beyond, "I haven't reviewed this book because I thought it was a manual for bricklayers." Vela, offended by this, wrote a more positive review for *El Universal Ilustrado*, the weekly supplement to the newspaper where he worked, *El Universal*. Two months later, that paper published an interview with Maples under the headline "Our Creationist Apostle." Two months after that, again in the same paper, a survey of Mexican literati asked "Who is the worst writer in Mexico?" The most frequent response given, by a wide margin, was Manuel Maples Arce.

The Mexican literary establishment was quite simply completely unprepared for Stridentism. Maples hit them with fully developed avant-garde aesthetics, and it seems to have been the first time many of them had ever heard of such a thing. *El Universal* was by no means the only publication that would praise Maples in one issue and trash him in the next. But for Maples more than most, there was no such thing as bad press. It did what he hoped it would: drove conversation, kept his name in the papers, sold books, and brought other brash writers to his side. Both Arqueles Vela and List Arzubide, for example, came to Stridentism as a direct result of the scandal around *Inner Scaffolds*. The opinions of literati in general, as they did elsewhere the avant-garde appeared, split along generational lines. The older, more established writers hated it more than anything they had ever seen. The younger, less established ones thought it was the greatest thing that ever happened. And they gathered not so much around Maples as with him.

These were heady days and, by all accounts except his own, Maples reveled in them. He and the Stridentists took up residence in a Mexico City café, which they unilaterally renamed the Café Nobody. There they held court and planned their next provocation/publicity stunt. One of their favorite and most effective methods was simply insulting other poets, which they did often and with gusto. This frequently got the results they sought. An anecdote List Arzubide told Bolaño, about the aftermath of the release of one of their later manifestos, is typical:

Manuel and I were walking along when we saw one of the poets we'd alluded to, Gabriel Sánchez Guerrero, who was very nearsighted, surrounded by three or four others reading that broadsheet (since he was very nearsighted he almost had it stuck to his face), and someone told him that I was coming: then he lowered it and insulted me. He said, "I'm going to answer this as it deserves, possibly by insulting your mother," and I said to him, well, then you're going to have to start with me and we can take it from there. Then everybody got riled up, and Manuel leaned back like so, back then he wore gaiters and always carried his cane, and he said those famous words: "Stridentism doesn't take IOUs or offer credit, and you, sir, are a literary potlicker." Some guy who was there jumped on top of me and tried to hit me with his cane, I raised my arm and gave him a slap and they separated us and Maples and I continued our walk, apparently very calm.

Of course, none of this would have been possible if Maples's poems didn't work or didn't do what he said they should. The poems in *Inner Scaffolds* did both. Scandalously abandoning the very things that had made older poetry poetic (formal meter and rhyming patterns, "proper" themes), they introduced a free-verse structure, abandoned rhyme, and rested on a foundation of thematic elements drawn from real, modern life. While their use of such borderline poetic clichés as souls and flowers dates them somewhat now, it was the use of such familiar imagery that, by contrast, drew attention to what was new in the poems: their form and their use of modern subjects like airplanes and alienation.

Two years later, in 1924, the core of the Stridentist movement had formed. Importantly, it contained more than just poets and prose writers, but quite a large number of visual artists as well. Among them were French expat Jean Charlot, who specialized in woodcuts, the sculptor and mask maker Germán Cueto, and painters Ramón Alva de la Canal and Fermín Revueltas. Many others were closely affiliated with Stridentism, some so much so that one could argue for their status as members of the group, including such well-known figures as Frida Kahlo, Diego Riviera, Edward Weston, and Tina Modotti. And when prominent avant-gardists such as Sergei Eisenstein and John Dos Passos came to Mexico, it was Maples and the Stridentists they hung out with.

Many, perhaps most, of the people involved in Stridentism at this time were members of the Communist Party of Mexico. Maples, unlike virtually all of his associates, was not working class. He was a lawyer, and quite visibly petty bourgeois in his dress and mannerisms: pomaded hair, well-tailored suit and kid gloves, gaiters, expensive shoes and cane, flower in his lapel, very fast motorcycle and a (probably exaggerated) habit of never appearing in public with the same woman twice. Maples himself never joined the Party, and while the class dynamics within the group would eventually lead to its breakup, he was at this time at the very least a serious fellow traveler. The best evidence for this is Maples's next book, published that year: CITY: *Bolshevik Superpoem in 5 Cantos*.

For Arqueles Vela, "CITY is *the* poem of the Mexican Revolution." That is hard to argue with. Much of the best literature on the subject, such as the work of Mariano Azuela and Juan Rulfo, is prose. Poets of the time did not seem to notice much of what, by 1924, had been going on around them for many, many years. Which was the point Maples and the Stridentists were trying to make. Mexico had gone through a revolution, which had tapered off by 1924 but wasn't really over. As the violence began to subside, modernization was introduced. The country was filling up, especially in the larger cities, with cars, airplanes, radios, skyscrapers, electricity, trains, cinema. These were not merely cool curios, but the result of fundamental political changes in the structure of Mexican society. And the mainstream poets of the day were still partying like it was 1899. This was a political choice, one that the Stridentists, whose work was an expression of an opposing political choice, wanted not to critique but destroy.

Very little avant-garde art during this period, outside of the Soviet Union, was as overtly political as Stridentism. Tina Modotti's famous hammer, sickle, and sombrero photograph dates from this period, and sets a standard that CITY (along with other Stridentist work) easily meets. CITY makes no attempt to do anything but flaunt its politics, but if it is "propaganda" it is an exceptionally opaque example. The revolution in CITY is protean: a city at one point, a woman at another, then a mass of striking workers or a train full of revolutionary soldiers. Taken as a whole, CITY is a meditation on what revolution is, what it was in the Mexico of that time, and what was lost, even in apparent victory. I have no hesitation naming it among the finest pieces of communist art ever produced, an equal to the work of Mayakovsky, Modotti, Cortázar, and Gorky.

Stridentism was soon to become yet more political. In December 1924, General Heriberto Jara became governor of the Mexican state of Veracruz. A clue to Jara's politics is the fact that, in its inaugural year of 1950, he was awarded the International Stalin Prize. Later renamed the International Lenin Peace Prize, this was the Soviet answer to the Nobel Peace Prize. Future recipients included Du Bois, Picasso, Castro, Salvador Allende, Angela Davis, and Nelson Mandela. In 1925, Jara appointed Maples Arce as a judge, which was reasonable enough given that Maples was a practicing lawyer who shared the General's political views.

At this point, Stridentism effectively relocated to Veracruz. There, it entered its most intense and, as it turned out, final phase. List Arzubide published his major poetry collection of the period in 1925, and a history of Stridentism (which was also another manifesto) the following year. Vela published a prose collection named after the Café Nobody. All the visual artists in the group produced major works of their own. And the whole movement collaborated on their most ambitious, most controversial, least understood project of all: the creation of their own city, Stridentopolis.

This project has, justifiably, become a major focus in studies of Stridentism. How serious were they? Was this a plan for a real city, some kind of vast game of exquisite corpse, or what? On the one hand, actual plans *were* drawn up for individual buildings and whole neighborhoods, and a lot of writing was devoted to imaging Stridentopolis, its spaces, and daily life there. On the other hand, the whole idea was obviously maniacal. The difficulty in answering this question is part of what makes the idea so compelling. But whatever else it might have been, Stridentopolis was obviously an early experiment in the kind of theoretical urbanism and psychogeography that would preoccupy Guy Debord and the Situationists four decades later.

Of course, the question of the Stridentists' intent in this matter would be moot without the political power and resources to actually break ground. But in 1926, Stridentism did in fact gain at least some access to such power and resources, when General Jara promoted Maples to General Secretary of the Government, one of the most powerful positions in the state. How'd that go? Well, in October 1927, Jara was removed from power in a de facto coup by opponents who cited his relationship with Stridentism as one of their major justifications. This had, they argued, led to a "Stridentification" of Veracruz that they could not tolerate. It seems highly likely that the apparent seriousness of the Stridentopolis project, and Maples's high position in the government, were at least excuses if not factors for the fall of Jara's government.

As these events were in motion, Maples published the last of his Stridentist books, 1927's *Prohibited Poems*. More a collection of poems than his two prior efforts, this book contains some of Maples's finest, most progressive work. The poems are much more refined than those in *Inner Scaffolds*, incorporating the stylistic breakthroughs of *CITY* into discrete lyrics that lack the dated tropes of the earlier work. It is perhaps the finest work of his entire career, though Maples himself would probably have disagreed. He would not publish another book of his own poems for twenty years.

While the removal of General Jara from power made Veracruz untenable as a home for Stridentism, it was Maples himself who made Stridentism untenable as a movement. Rather than return to Mexico City or relocate with the group elsewhere, Maples simply left the country, studying diplomatic law at the Sorbonne and then entering the diplomatic corps. The other Stridentists, not one of whom had anything like Maples's financial resources or connections to the establishment, remained in Mexico. Virtually all of them went on making avant-garde art and literature, and some became much more involved in the Communist Party. The mood among the group towards Maples's departure was captured again in *Los detectives salvajes*, in a passage narrated by a character based on List Arzubide:

> One morning, reading the newspaper, I learned that he had left for Europe. The poet Manuel Maples Arce, it said, left Veracruz bound for Le Havre. It didn't say the father of Stridentism had left for Europe or the first Mexican avant-garde poet had set out for the Old Continent, but simply: the poet Manuel Maples Arce. And maybe it didn't even say the poet, maybe the paper said the lawyer Maples Arce has left for a French port, where he will continue by other means (by runaway train!) his voyage to Italian soil, where he will take up the post of consul or vice-consul or cultural attaché at the Mexican embassy in Rome.

In 1940, while attached to the embassy in Rome, Maples edited an *Anthology of Modern Mexican Poetry*. His own poems appeared in it, of course. What did not appear in it, anywhere, even once, was the word "Stridentism." And neither did any member of the movement other than himself. Germán List Arzubide lived to be one hundred, an active Party member the entire time, and at various times expressed the view shared by others: that Maples did not just walk away, but took refuge in the privileges of his class when Stridentism's political situation became difficult. That he did not simply abandon his friends and the work they had done together, but went further, attempting to erase Stridentism altogether, not only from his own biography but from history itself. And laying aside the bitterness of feeling, which is itself fairly eloquent, the record not only supports this view, but suggests that he went on with these efforts until the 1970s, when revived interest in Stridentism made such erasure impossible—at which point he simply resumed trying to take all the credit for it himself, as he had in the twenties.

In the five decades that passed between his departure from Mexico and Bolaño's arrival at his home, Maples served in many diplomatic postings, including as ambassador to Canada and France. He published numerous volumes of poetry, criticism, and memoir. But nothing he did in those years had anything like the impact or importance of his Stridentist period, a fact that, if the way he treated Bolaño is any guide, he probably found very annoying.

— *KM Cascia*

Sources

Roberto Bolaño. "Tres Estridentistas en 1976." *Revista Plural* (November 1976).

——. *Los detectives salvajes* (Anagrama, 1998)

Silvia Pappe. *Estridentópolis: urbanización y montaje* (Universidad Autonoma Metropolitana, 2014)

Luis Mario Schneider. *Estridentismo: Una literatura de estrategia* (Insituto Nacional de Bellas Artes, 1970)

——. *El estridentismo: México, 1921-1927* (UNAM, 1985)

All translations are my own.

MANUEL MAPLES ARCE

STRIDENTIST POEMS

ANDAMIOS INTERIORES:

POEMAS RADIOGRÁFICOS

INNER SCAFFOLDS:

RADIOGRAPHIC POEMS

1922

*Verdadero artista es el hombre que
cree absolutamente en sí, porque él
es absolutamente él mismo.*

Oscar Wilde

The true artist is he who
believes in himself absolutely,
because he is absolutely himself.

Oscar Wilde

*A la que sacudió sobre mi vida
una primavera de alas.*

To she who shook a
winged spring over my life

Ex-libris

Ex-libris

Prisma

Yo soy un punto muerto en medio de la hora,
equidistante al grito náufrago de una estrella.
Un parque de manubrio se engarrota en la sombra,
y la luna sin cuerda
me oprime en las vidrieras.

                        Margaritas de oro
                        deshojadas al viento.
La ciudad insurrecta de anuncios luminosos
flota en los almanaques
y allá de tarde en tarde,
por la calle planchada se desangra en eléctrico.

El insomnio, lo mismo que una enredadera,
se abraza a los andamios sinoples de telégrafo,
y mientras que los ruidos descerrajan las puertas,
la noche ha enflaquecido lamiendo su recuerdo.

El silencio amarillo suena sobre mis ojos.
Prismal, diáfana mía, para sentirlo todo!

Yo departí sus manos,
pero en aquella hora
grís de las estaciones,
sus palabras mojadas se me echaron al cuello,
y una locomotora
sedienta de kilómetros la arrancó de mis brazos.

Hoy suenan sus palabras más heladas que nunca,
y la locura de Edison a manos de la lluvia!

El cielo es un obstáculo para el hotel inverso
refractado en las lunas sombrías de los espejos;

Prism

I'm a still point in the middle of the moment,
equidistant to a star's castaway shout.
A handlebarred park goes shadow numb,
the wound-down moon
oppresses me in shop windows.
                              Golden daisies
                              wind-plucked.
Rebel city of luminous news
afloat in almanacs,
and where, from time to time,
electricity bleeds in the ironed street.

Insomnia, like a vine,
embraces vert telegraph scaffolds,
and noises pick locks while
night grows thin licking memory.

Yellow silence sounds over my eyes.
Prismal, my diaphonous one, to feel everything!

I left her hands,
but in that gray
train station hour,
her wet words were flung at me,
and a locomotive,
thirsty for distance, snatched her from my arms.

Today her words sound more frozen than ever,
Edison's madness in hands of rain!

The sky an obstacle for an inverted hotel
refracted in shadowed mirror moons;

los violines se suben como la champaña,
y mientras las ojeras sondean la madrugada,
el invierno huesoso tirita en los percheros.

Mis nervios se derraman.
                              La estrella del recuerdo
naufragada en el agua
del silencio.

              Tú y yo

                                        coincidimos
                                        en la noche terrible,
meditación temática
deshojada en jardines.

Locomotoras, gritos,
arsenales, telégrafos.

El amor y la vida
son hoy sindicalistas,

y todo se dilata en círculos concéntricos.

violins rise like champagne,
and while ears hear early morning,
bony winter shivers on coat racks.

My nerves pour out.
            Memory's star
shipwrecked in water
of silence.

       You and I,

             coincide
             in terrible night,
meditation on a theme
plucked bare in gardens.

Locomotives, shouts,
arsenals, telegraphs.

Love and life
today for Labor,

and everything expands in concentric circles.

Flores aritméticas

Arithmetic Flowers

Esas rosas eléctricas...

Esas rosas eléctricas de los cafés con música
que estilizan sus noches con "poses" operísticas,
languidecen de muerte, como las semifusas,
en tanto que en la orquesta se encienden anilinas
y bosteza la sífilis entre "tubos de estufa".

Equivocando un salto de trampolín, las joyas
se confunden estrellas de catálogos Osram.

Y olvidado en el hombro de alguna Margarita,
deshojado por todos los poetas franceses,
me galvanizauna de estas pálidas "ísticas"
que desvelan de balde sus ojeras dramáticas,
y un recuerdo de otoño de hospital se me entibia.

Y entre sorbos de exóticos nombres fermentados,
el amor, que es un fácil juego de cubilete,
prende en una absurda figura literaria
el dibujo melódico de un vals incandescente.

El violín se accidenta en sollozos teatrales,
y se arragante un pájaro los últimos compases.

Este techo se llueve.
La noche en el jardín
se da toques con pilas eléctricas de éter,
y la luna está al último grito de París.

Y en la sala ruidosa,
el mesero académico deshorchaba las horas.

Those electric roses...

Those electric roses in music cafés,
that stylize nights with opera poses,
languish in death, like sixty-fourth notes,
while the orchestra lights aniline on fire
and syphilis yawns through "stove pipes."

Mistaken trampoline jump, jewels
confused with stars from Osram's catalogue.

And, forgotten on the shoulder of some Daisy,
plucked bare by all the French poets,
I'm galvanized by one of those pale "istics"
that keep dramatic ears awake without reason,
warmed by the memory of autumn hospital.

And between exotic sips of fermented names,
love, a simple dice game,
lights, an absurd literary figure,
the melodic sketch of an incandescent waltz.

The violin crashes in theatrical sobs,
and a bird chokes the last few beats.

The roof is raining.
Garden night flickers
electric ether batteries,
and Paris' last scream is that moon.

In the noisy dining room,
an academic waiter uncorks hours.

Todo en un plano oblicuo...

En tanto que la tisis -todo en un plano oblicuo-
paseante de automóvil y tedio triangular,
me electrizó en el vértice agudo de mí mismo.
Van callendo las horas de un modo vertical.

Y simultaneizada bajo la sombra eclíptica
de aquel sombrero unánime,
se ladea una sonrisa,
mientras que la blancura en éxtasis de frasco
se envuelve en una llama d'Orsay de gasolina.
          Me debrayo en un claro
          de anuncio cinemático.

Y detrás de la lluvia que peinó los jardines
hay un hervor galante de encajes auditivos;
a aquel violín morado le operan la laringe
y una estrella reciente se desangra en suspiros.

Un incendio de aplausos consume las lunetas
de la clínica, y luego -oh ánonima de siempre-
desvistiendo sus laxas indolencias modernas,
reincide -flor de lucro- tras los impertinentes.
          Pero todo esto es sólo
          un efecto cinemático,

porque ahora, siguiendo el entierro de coches,
allá de tarde en tarde estornuda un voltáico
sobre las caras lívidas de los "players" románticos,
y florecen algunos aeroplanos de hidrógeno.

Entirely on an oblique plane...

When consumption—entirely on an oblique plane—
passed by in a car and triangular boredom,
it electrified my acute vertex.
The hours go on in vertical fall.

And at the same time, under the ecliptic shadow
of that unanimous hat,
a smile tilts,
while whiteness in bottled ecstasy
wraps whiteness in d'Orsay gasoline flame.
        I get lost in a clearing
        in cinematic news.

And there's a gallant fervor of listening lace
behind rain-combed gardens:
an operation on a bruised violin throat
and blood sighs from a fresh star.

Applause fire consumes clinic
lunatics, and then—oh ever anonymous—
undressing indolent modern laxness,
relapses—profit flower—behind impertinence.
        But all this is just
        cinematic effect,

because now, after auto burials,
a battery sneezes now and then
in livid faces of romantic players,
and hydrogen airships blossom.

En la esquina, un "umpire" de tráfico, a su modo,
va midiendo los "outs", y en este amarillismo,
se promulga un sistema luminista de rótulos.

Por la calle verdosa hay brumas de suicidio.

On the corner, traffic umpires
tally outs, like they do, this sensationalism
spreads a luminous system of signs.

Suicide mist in greenish streets.

A veces, con la tarde...

A veces, con la tarde luida de los bordes
un fracaso de alas se barre en el jardín.
Y mientras que la vida esquina a los relojes,
se pierdan por la acera los pasos de la noche.

Amarillismo
gris.

Mis ojos deletrean la ciudad algebráica
entre las subversiones de los escaparates;
detrás de los tranvías se explican las fachadas
y las alas del viento se rompen en los cables.

Siento íntegro toda la instalación estética
lateral a las calles alambradas de ruido,
que quiebran sobre el piano sus manos antisépticas,
y luego se recogen en un libro mullido.

A través del insomnio centrado en las ventanas
trepidan los andamios de una virginidad,
y al final de un acceso paroxista de lágrimas,
llamas de podredumbre suben del bulevard.

Y equivocadamente, mi corazón payaso,
se engolfa entre nocturnos encantos de a 2 pesos;
amor, mi vida, etc., y algún coche reumático
sueña con un voltáico que le asesina el sueño.

Sometimes, in edge-rubbed afternoons...

Sometimes, in edge-rubbed afternoons,
wing failure sweeps the garden.
And while life corners clocks,
night steps get lost on pavement.

                    Gray
                    sensationalism.

My eyes spell the algebraic city
through shop window subversions;
behind streetcars, facades explain
and wind's wings break against cables.

Aesthetic installations feel unabriged
beside noise-fenced streets,
antiseptic hands break over the piano,
and get gathered into a soft book.

Through window-centered insomnia
virginity scaffolds tremble,
and after a spasm of tears,
decay flames climb the boulevard.

And mistakenly, my clownish heart
throws itself into 2 peso night enchantments:
love, my life, etc., and some rheumatic car
dreams of a battery that murders sleep.

Sombra laboratorio. Las cosas bajo sobre,
ventilador eléctrico, champagne + F. T.
Marinetti = a

                         Nocturno futurista
                         1912.

Y 200 estrellas de vicio a flor de noche
escupen pendejadas y besos de papel.

Shadow laboratory. Things low overhead.
Electric fan, champagne + F.T.
Marinetti =

>Futurist nocturne
>1912.

And 200 vice stars in heart of night
spit bullshit and paper kisses.

Voces amarillas

Yellow Voices

Y nada de hojas secas...

(La mañana romántica, como un ruido espumoso,
se derrama en la calle de este barrio incoloro
por donde a veces pasan repartiendo programas,
y es una clara música que se oye con los ojos
la palidez enferma de la super-amada.

En tanto que un poeta,
colgado en la ventana,
se muere haciendo gárgaras
de plata
electrizada,

subido a los peldañas de una escalera
cromática,
barnizo sus dolencias con vocablos azules,
y anclada en un letargo de cosas panorámicas,
su vida se evapora lo mismo que un perfume.)

—Mi tristeza de antes es la misma de hoy.
—Tú siempre con tus cosas.

                      —Oh poeta, perdón.
(En el jardín morado
se rompe el equilibrio fragante de una flor.)

—Sol, blancura, etc., y nada de hojas secas.
—La vida es sólo un grito que se me cuelga al cuello
lo mismo que un adiós.
                 —Hablemos de otra cosa,
te lo ruego.

And no dry leaves...

(Romantic morning, like foamy noise,
spills in colorless neighborhood streets
where sometimes they hand out programs,
and a well-loved girl's sickly paleness
is a clear music heard with eyes.

While a poet,
hung in the window,
dies gargling
electrified
silver,

climbs the steps of a chromatic scale,
varnishes ailments in blue words
and, anchored in lethargy of scenic things,
his life evaporates like perfume.)

—My sadness today is the same as yesterday.
—You're always carrying on.

                    —Oh poet, excuse me!

(In purple garden
fragrant flower balance breaks.)

—Sun, whiteness, etc., and no dry leaves.
—Life's just a scream that hangs from my neck
like a goodbye.
                    —Let's talk about something else,
I beg you.

       (Su voz
tiene dobleces románticos de felpa
que estuvo mucho tiempo guardada en naftalina,
y duerme en sus cansancios ingrávidos de enferma,
la elegancia de todas las cosas amarillas.

Y mientras la mañana, atónita de espejos,
estalla en el alféizar de la hora vulgar,
el dolor se derrama, lo mismo que un tintero,
sobre la partitura de su alma musical.)

(Her voice
has romantic folds like plush
stored in mothballs a long time,
and elegance of all these yellow things
sleeps in her sick woman's weightless exhaustion.

And while the morning, amazed by mirrors,
crashes into the window sill at the usual hour,
pain spills, like an inkwell,
over the music to her melodious soul.)

En la dolencia estática

(En la dolencia estática de este jardín mecánico,
el olor de las horas huele a convalecencia,
y el pentagrama eléctrico de todos los tejados
se muere en el alero del último almanaque.

Extraviada en maneras musicales de enferma
inmoviliza un sueño su vertical blancura,
en tanto que un obscuro violín de quinto piso
se deshoja a lo largo de un poema de Schumann,
y en todos los periódicos se ha suicidado un tísico.)

—Hoy pasan los entierros, como un cuento de ojeras,
lo mismo que en otoño.
    —Ese tema, no es tema
de primavera. Ya ves lo que dice el médico!

(En el jardín hay 5 centavos de silencio.)

—Entonces, quiero un poco de sol azucarado.
—Ya vuelves con tu acústica.
    —Pues mírame las manos.
Mis dedos caligráficos se han vuelto endecasílabos.

(Y meditando un lento compás de 3 por 4.)

—¡Oh tus cosas melódicas!
    —¡Soy un frasco de música!—

(Y en esta tarde lírica
    85-74 señorita...

In the ecstatic ailment...

(In this mechanical garden's static ailment,
hours smell of convalescence,
and the electric treble clef of every rooftop
dies in the last almanac eaves.

Lost in a sick woman's musical ways,
a dream stills her vertical whiteness,
while an obscure fifth-floor violin
rips petals off a Schumann poem,
and in every paper, a consumptive killed himself.)

—The funerals are today, as an excuse for tired eyes,
same as in autumn.
                —This conversation, it's not a spring
conversation. Now you see what the doctor says!

(In the garden there are 5 centavos of silence.)

—Then, I want a little sugared sun.
—Now here you come with your acoustics.
                —Well look at my hands.
My calligraphic fingers have turned to endecasyllables.

(And thinking about a slow 3/4 beat:)

—You and your melodic whatnots!
                —I'm a musical failure!—

(And in this lyric afternoon
                85-74, lady...

la primavera pasa como en motocicleta,
y al oro moribundo, historiada de cintas,
lo mismo que un refajo se seca mi tristeza.)

spring passes as on a motorcycle
and in dying gold, done up in ribbons,
my sadness dries like a petticoat.)

Por las horas de cuento...

Por las horas de cuento de estos parques sin rosas,
abulan, un diptongo de ensueño, nuestras sombras.

Y en tanto que algún piano fantástico, desvela
los bemoles románticos de un estudio sin luna,
sus ojos se adormecen en un cansancio felpa,
como si se estuviera muriendo de blancura.

(Y después, quedamente;)
        —¿Amor, oyes las hojas?
—¡Si no es eso!
        —¿Entonces?
        —Tal vez es una enferma
que llora con Beethoven...

(Y seguimos del brazo nuestro obscuro diptongo,
por los parques afónicos,
lacrimeantes de oro...)

—¡Me quisiera morir!
        —¡No digas esas cosas
que me hacen tanto mal!
        —¡Si la vida is tan triste!
—Pero no pienses eso.
        —¡Si la vida es tan triste!
—Me duele el corazón cuando tú estás así.

Doblaremos la hoja.

        (Y sobre el mismo tema,
su voz, casi ojerosa,)

At story time...

At story time in roseless parks,
they wander, a dream diphthong, our shadows.

And while some fantastic piano keeps
romantic b-flats awake in a moonless studio,
her eyes doze in plush weariness,
as though dying of whiteness.

(And then, quietly:)
           —Love, do you hear the leaves?
—It's not that!
      —Then?
          —Maybe it's a sick woman
weeping over Beethoven...

(And arm in arm follow our dark diphthong,
through mute parks,
golden tearful...)

—I want to die!
          —Don't say such things,
they hurt me so!
          —Life is so sad!
—But don't think that.
          —Life is so sad!
—My heart hurts when you're like this.

We fold the leaf.

          (And on the same subject,
her voice, almost with crow's feet:)

—¡Me quisiera morir!
¡Me quisiera morir!

(Y en el cloroformado cansancio de la sombra,
nuestras 2 vidas juntas, por el parque sin rosas,
se pierden en la noche romántica de otoño
ambulando en silencio la teoría de un diptongo.)

     —I want to die!
I want to die!

(And in shadow's chloroformed weariness,
our 2 lives together, through the roseless park,
get lost in romantic autumn night,
diphthong theory wandering in silence.)

Perfumes Apagados

Lifeless Perfumes

Al margen de la lluvia...

Al margen de la lluvia en los cafés insomnes,
los perfiles se duermen en las láminas sordas.
Y es ahora que todo coincide en los relojes,
mi corazón nostálgico ardiéndose en la sombra.

Después de los vulgares asombros del periódico
en que sólo se oye el humo de las pipas,
florecen a intervalos las actitudes lividas
retropróximamente de los paraguas cónicos.

Deduzco de la lluvia que esto es definitivo.
¿Quién está en el manubrio? Hay un corto circuito.

La trama es complicado siniestro de oficina,
y algunas señoritas,
literalmente teóricas,
se han vuelto perifrásticas, ahora en re bemol,
con abandonos táctiles sobre el papel de lija.

Explotan las estrellas
eléctricas en flor.

Pero más que todo esto, en el sintaxicidio
de unos cuantos renglones desgarrados de adioses,
¡oh su carne amarilla!
¡mis dedos retroactivos!

   (En el piano automático
   se va haciendo de noche.)

Y en el mismo declive del interior romántico
me interrumpo en un faro de automóvil, en tanto,

On rain's edge...

On rain's edge, in café insomnia,
profiles sleep in deaf illustration.
Now everything coincides in clocks:
my nostalgic heart burns in shadow.

After vulgar newspaper wonders
where only pipesmoke is heard,
livid attitudes of conical umbrellas
at intervals retrosuddenly bloom.

I deduce from the rain, this is definitive.
Who's at the controls? There's a short circuit.

The plot a complicated office disaster,
and some young ladies,
literally theoretical,
have become paraphrases, now in d-flat,
with tactile abandon over sandpaper.

Flowering electric
stars explode.

But more than this, in the syntaxicide
of a few torn up lines of goodbyes:
oh yellow flesh!
my retroactive fingers!

       (Night falls on the
       automatic piano.)

In exactly an inner romantic's decline
I interrupt myself in headlights, while

—bohemios romboidales— mi corazon se llueve;
la tarde en las vidrieras traquetea como un tren,
y mi dolor naufraga, definitivamente
en la literatura de todos los "ayer".

—rhomboidal bohemias—my heart rains;
afternoon clatters on windows like a train,
and my pain sinks, definitively,
in the literature of every "yesterday."

Como una gotera...

Como una gotera de cristal, su recuerdo,
agujera el silencio
de mis días amarillos.

Tramitamos palabras
por sellos de correo,
y la vida automática
se asolea en los andamios de un vulgar rotativo.

Las canciones florecen
a través de la lluvia,
en la tarde vacía, sin teclado y sin lagrimas.

Los tranvías se llevaron las calles cinemáticas
empapeladas de ventanas.

Mis besos apretados
florecían en su carne.

Aquel adiós, el último,
fue un grito sin salida.

La ciudad paroxista
nos llegaba hasta el cuello,
y un final de kilómetros subrayó sus congojas.

¡Oh el camino de hierro!
              un incendio de alas
              a través del telégrafo.
              Trágicas chimeneas
              agujeran el cielo.

Like a leak...

Like a crystal leak, her memory,
pierces silence
of yellow days.

We deal with words
by postage stamp,
and automated life
suns on a printer's scaffold.

Songs flower
by means of rain,
in empty afternoon, no keyboard, no tears.

Streetcars carry cinematic streets
papered with windows.

My pressed kisses
flowered on her flesh.

That goodbye, the last one,
was a dead-end cry.

The paroxysist city
comes up to our necks,
an ending of distance underlines our distress.

Oh iron road!
   Wing fire
   via telegraph.
   Tragic chimneys
   pierce the sky.

¡Y el humo de las fábricas!

(Así, todo, de lejos, se me dice como algo
imposible que nunca he tenido en las manos.)

Un piano tangencial se acomoda en la sombra
del jardín inconcreto; los interiores todos
se exponen a la lluvia—selecciones de ópera—.
en las esquinas nórdicas hay manifiestos rojos.

And factory smoke!

(So, everything, far, speaks to me like
impossible something, never held.)

Tangential piano settles in abstract
garden shadow; interiors all
exposed to rain—opera selections.
Red manifestos on Nordic corners.

Tras los adioses últimos...

Tardes alcanforadas en vidrieras de enfermo,
tras los adioses últimos de las locomotoras,
y en las palpitaciones cardíacas del pañuelo
hay un desgarramiento de frases espasmódicas.

El ascensor eléctrico y un piano intermitente
complican el sistema de la casa de "apartments",
y en el grito morado de los últimos trenes
intuyo la distancia.

A espaldas de la ausencia se demuda el telégrafo.
Despachos emotivos desangran mí interior.

Sugerencia, L-10 y recortes de periódico,
oh dolorosa mía,
tú estás lejos de todo,
y estas horas que caen amarillean la vida.

En el fru-fru inalámbrico de vestido automático
que enreda por la casa su pauta seccional,
incodo sobre un éxtasis de sol a las vidrieras,
y la ciudad es una ferretería espectral.

　　　Las canciones domésticas
　　　de codos a la calle.

(Ella era un desmayo de prestigios supremos
y dolencias católicas de perfumes envueltos
a través de mis dedos!)

After the last goodbyes...

Camphored afternoons in sickness windows,
after last locomotive goodbyes,
and tearing of spasmodic phrases
in a handkerchief's cardiac palpitations.

Electric elevator and intermittent piano
complicate the building's system,
and in last train purple shouts
I intuit distance.

Behind absence's back telegraph alters.
Emotive departments bleed my innards.

Suggestion, L-10 and newspaper clippings;
oh painful lady,
you're far from everything,
these fallen hours yellow life.

In wireless rustle the automatic dress
tangles the house in segmented line,
I affect sun ecstasy in windows,
and the city is a spectral ironmonger.

> Domestic songs
> of elbows in the street.

(She was a fainting of supreme prestige
and Catholic perfume ailments wrapped
around my fingers.)

Accidente de lágrimas. Locomotoras últimas
renegridas a fuerza de gritarnos adiós,
y ella en 3 latitudes, ácida de blancura,
derramada en silencio sobre mi corazón.

Accident of tears. Last locomotives
black from shouting goodbye to us,
and she in 3 latitudes, whiteness acid,
spilled in silence over my heart.

URBE:

SUPER-POEMA BOLCHEVIQUE

EN 5 CANTOS

CITY:

BOLSHEVIK SUPER-POEM

IN 5 CANTOS

1924

A los obreros de México

To the workers of Mexico

I

He aquí mi poema
brutal
y multánime
a la nueva ciudad.

Oh ciudad toda tensa
de cables y de esfuerzos,
sonora toda
de motores y de alas.

Explosión simultánea
de las nuevas teorías
un poco más allá
En el plano espacial
de Whitman y de Turner
y un poco más acá
de Maples Arce.

Los pulmones de Rusia
soplan hacia nosotros
el viento de la revolución social.
Los asalta braguetas literarios
nada comprenderán
de esta nueva belleza
sudorosa del siglo,
y las lunas
maduras
que cayeron,
son esta podredumbre
que nos llega
de las atarjeas intelectuales.

I

Here's my brutal
many-minded
poem
to the new city.

        Oh city all tense
        with wires and effort,
        all noisy
        with motors and wings.

        Explosion of the new
        theories combined,
        a little further
On the spatial plane
        from Whitman and Turner,
        a little closer
        to Maples Arce.

Russia's lungs
blow the wind
of social revolution
in our direction.
Literary dick gropers
will understand nothing
about the century's
sweating new beauty,
        and the fallen
        ripe
        moons,
        they are that rot
        that reaches us
        from intellectual sewers.

He aquí mi poema:

> Oh ciudad fuerte
> y múltiple,
> hecha toda de hierro y de acero.

Los muelles. Las dársenas.
Las grúas.

> *Y la fiebre sexual*
de las fábricas.

> Urbe:
>> Escoltas de tranvías
>> que recorren las calles subversivas.
>> Los escaparates asaltan las aceras,
>> y el sol, saquea las avenidas.
>> Al márgen de los días
>> tarifados de postes telefónicos
>> desfilan paisajes momentáneos
>> por sistemas de tubos ascensores.

Súbitamente,
oh el fogonazo
verde de sus ojos.
Bajo las persianas ingenuas de la hora
pasan los batallones rojos.
El romanticismo caníbal de la música yanke
ha ido haciendo sus nidos en los mástiles.
Oh ciudad internacional,
¿hacia qué remoto meridiano
cortó aquel trasatlántico?
Yo siento que se aleja todo.
Los crepúsculos ajados
flotan entre la mampostería del panorama.
Trenes espectrales que van
hacia allá

Here's my poem:

> Oh strong,
> numerous city
> entirely made of iron and concrete.

The piers. The docks.
The cranes.

> *And the sexual fever*
of factories.

> City:
>> Bodyguard streetcars
>> patrol subversive streets.
>> Shop windows assault sidewalks,
>> and the sun sacks avenues.
>> On the margins of days
>> taxed with telephone poles,
>> momentary landscapes march through
>> a system of ascending tubes.

Suddenly,
oh the green
flash of her eyes.
Red battalions pass under
the naïve shutters of the times.
Yankee music's cannibal romanticism
has built nests on the masts.
Oh international city,
to what remote meridian did that
transatlantic ship sail?
I feel everything moving away.
Wrinkled evenings
float among the scene's masonry.
Spectral trains go
far

lejos, jadeantes de civilizaciones.

La multitud desencajada
chapotea musicalmente en la calles.

Y ahora, los burgueses ladrones, se echarán a temblar
por los caudales
que robaron al pueblo,
pero alguien ocultó bajo sus sueños
el pentagrama espiritual del explosivo.

He aquí mi poema:

Gallardetes de hurras al viento,
cabelleras incendiadas
y mañana cautivas en los ojos.

Oh ciudad
musical
hecha toda de ritmos mecánicos.

Mañana, quizás,
sólo la lumbre viva de mis versos
alumbrará los horizontes humillados.

II

Esta nueva profundidad del panorama
es una proyección hacia los espejismos interiores.

La muchedumbre sonora
hoy rebasa las plazas comunales

away, the panting of civilizations.

The unhinged masses
splash musically in the streets.

And now the thieving bourgeoisie will tremble
for their riches,
robbed from the people,
but someone hid the sheet music to
an explosion beneath their dreams.

Here's my poem:

Pennants of cheering in the wind,
hair on fire
and captive mornings in her eyes.

Oh musical
city
made entirely of mechanical rhythms.

Tomorrow, perhaps,
only the living fire of my verses
will light these humbled horizons.

II

This new depth in the scene
is a projection toward inner illusions.

Today the resounding crowd
floods the public squares

y los hurras triunfales
del obregonismo
reverberan al sol de las fachadas.

Oh muchacha romántica
flamarazo de oro.

Tal vez entre mis manos
sólo quedaron los momentos vivos.

Los paisajes vestidos de amarillo
se durmieron detrás de los cristales,
y la ciudad, arrebatada,
se ha quedado temblando en los cordajes.
Los aplausos son aquella muralla.

—¡Dios mío!

—No temas, es la ola romántica de las multitudes.
Después, sobre los desbordes del silencio,
la noche tarahumara irá creciendo.

Apaga tus vidrieras.
Entre la maquinaria del insomnio
la lujuria, son millones de ojos
que se untan en la carne.
Un pájaro de acero
ha emprotado su norte hacia una estrella

El puerto:

lejanías incendiadas,
el humo de las fábricas.
Sobre los tendederos de la música
se asolea su recuerdo.

and the triumphant shouts
of Obregonism
reflect the sun from the facades.

Oh romantic girl
blaze of gold.

    Maybe living moments were
    all that was left in my hands.

Landscapes dressed in yellow
fell asleep behind windows,
and the city, furious,
has been left trembling on the ropes.
That wall is the applause.

—My God!

    —Don't be afraid, it's the romantic wave of the masses.
Then, over the flooding silence,
the marathon night will rise.

        Darken your displays.
Lust in insomnia's
machinery, millions of eyes
spread themselves over flesh.
    A concrete bird
    has followed his own north toward a star.

The port:

    burning distances,
    factory smoke.
    Her memory hangs on
    clotheslines of music.

Un adios trasatlántico saltó desde la borda.

Los motores cantan
sobre el panorama muerto.

III

La tarde, acribillada de ventanas
flota sobre los hilos del teléfono,
y entre los atravesaños
inversos de la hora
se cuelgan los adioses de las máquinas.
   Su juventud maravillosa
   estalló una mañana
   entre mis dedos
   y en el agua, vacía,
   de los espejos,
   naufragaron los rostros olvidados.

Oh la pobre ciudad sindicalista
andamiada
de hurras y de gritos.

   Los obreros
   son rojos
   y amarillos.

Hay un florecimiento de pistolas
después del trampolín de los discursos,

A transatlantic farewell leapt from the deck.

Motors sing
over the dead scene.

III

Afternoon, riddled with windows,
floats over telephone wires,
and machine farewells
hang among the hour's
inverted crossbeams
  One morning her
  marvelous youth
  shattered
  in my hands,
  and forgotten faces
  sank into empty
  mirror waters.

Oh the poor union city
scaffolded
in cheers and shouts.

  The workers
  are red
  and yellow.

There's a flowering of pistols
after trampoline speeches,

y mientras los pulmones
del viento,
se supuran,
perdida en los obscuros pasillos de la música
alguna novia blanca
se deshoja.

IV

Entre los matorrales del silencio
la obscuridad lame la sangre del crepúsculo.
Las estrellas caídas,
son pájaros muertos
en el agua sin sueño
del espejo

Y las artillerías
sonoras del atlántico
se apagaron,
al fin,
en la distancia.

> Sobre la arboladura del otoño,
> sopla un viento nocturno:
> es el viento de Rusia,
> de las grandes tragedias,

y el jardín,
amarillo,
se va a pique en la sombra.
Súbito, su recuerdo,
chisporrotea en los interiores apagados.

and some white lover
lost in dark corridors of music
plucks her petals
while the lungs
of the wind
fester.

IV

In the scrublands of silence
darkness licks twilight's blood.
Fallen stars
are dead birds
in dreamless
mirror water.

And the Atlantic's
loud artilleries
go silent,
finally,
in the distance.

> A nocturnal wind blows
> over autumn's rigging:
> it's Russia's wind,
> the wind of great tragedies,

and the yellow
garden
falls apart in shadow,
Her sudden memory
casts sparks in inner darkness.

Sus palabras de oro
criban en mi memoria.

Los ríos de blusas azules
desbordan las esclusas de las fábricas,
y los árboles agitadores
manotean sus discursos en la acera.
Los huelguistas se arrojan
pedradas y denuestos,
y la vida, es una tumultuosa
conversión hacia la izquierda.

Al márgen de la almohada,
la noche, es un despeñadero;
y el insomnio,
se ha quedado escarbando en mi cerebro.

¿De quién son esas voces
que sobre nadan en la sombra?

      Y estos trenes que aullan
      hacia los horizontes devastados

      Los soladados,
      dormirán esta noche en el infierno

Dios mío,
y de todo este desastre
sólo unos cuantos pedazos
blancos,
de su recuerdo,
se me han quedado entre las manos.

My memory sifts through
her golden words.

Rivers of blue shirts
overflow the factory floodgates,
and rabble-rousing trees
punctuate sidewalk speeches with their hands.
Strikers throw
stones and insults,
and life is a raucous
conversion to the Left.

At the pillow's edge,
night is a precipice,
and insomnia
is still rummaging through my head.

Whose voices are those,
that swim in shadow above me?

And those trains that howl
toward wrecked horizons.

The soldiers,
they'll sleep in hell tonight.

My God,
and all that's left in my hands
from all this disaster
are a few
white pieces
of her memory.

V

Las hordas salvajes de la noche
se echaron sobre la ciudad amedrentada.

La bahía
florecida,
de mástiles y lunas,
se derrama
sobre la partitura
ingenua de sus manos,
y el grito, lejano
de un vapor,
hacia los mares nórdicos:

Adiós
al continente naufragado.

Entre los hilos de su nombre
se quedaron las plumas de los pájaros.

Pobre Celia María Dolores;
el panorama está dentro de nosotros.
Bajo los hachazos del silencio
las arquitecturas de hierro se devastan.

Hay oleadas de sangre y nubarrones de odio.

Desolación

Los discursos marihuanos
de los diputados
salpicaron de mierda su recuerdo,

V

The savage hordes of night
poured over the frightened city.

The bay,
blooming
with masts and moons,
pours
over her hands'
naïve orchestral score,
and the distant shout
of a steamship
headed for Nordic seas:

> Goodbye
> shipwrecked continent.

> Bird feathers hang
> in the wires of her name.

Poor Celia María Dolores;
the scene is inside us.
Iron architectures fall
under the axeblows of silence.

Waves of blood, storm clouds of hate.

> Desolation.

> Pothead speeches
> by politicians
> splatter her memory with shit,

pero,
sobre las multitudes de mi alma
se ha despeñado su ternura.

Ocotlán
allá lejos.

Voces

Los impactos picotean sobre
las trincheras.

La lujuria, apedreó toda la noche,
los balcones a oscuras de una virginidad.

La metralla
hace saltar pedazos del silencio.

Las calles
sonoras y desiertas,
son ríos de sombra
que van a dar al mar,
y el cielo, deshilachado,
es la nueva
bandera,
que flamea,
sobre la ciudad.

but
her tenderness has tripped over
my beloved masses
and fallen over a cliff.

Ocotlán
there in the distance.

Voices.

      Impacts pick over
      the trenches.

Lust threw stones all night
at the dark balconies of virginity.

Shrapnel
blows silence to pieces.

Noisy, deserted
streets
are shadow rivers
running to the sea,
and the unraveled sky
is the new flag
that flies
over the city.

POEMAS INTERDICTOS

PROHIBITED POEMS

1927

Canción desde un aeroplano

Estoy a la intemperie
de todas las estéticas;
operador siniestro
de los grandes sistemas,
tengo las manos
llenas
de azules continentes.

Aquí, desde esta borda,
esperaré la caída de las hojas.
La aviación
anticipa sus despojos,
y un puñado de pájaros
defiende su memoria.
Canción
florecida
de las rosas aéreas,
propulsión
entusiasta
de las hélices nuevas,
metáfora inefable despejada de alas.

Cantar
    Cantar.
Todo es desde arriba
equilibrado y superior,
y la vida
es el aplauso que resuena
en el hondo latido del avión.

Song from an airplane

I'm exposed to the elements
of all aesthetics;
sinister operator
of great systems,
my hands are
full
of blue continents.

Here, from this deck,
I'll wait for leaves to fall.
Aviation
hurries their removal,
a handful of birds
defends their memory.

Flowered
song
of aerial roses,
enthusiastic
propulsion
of new propellers,
ineffable clear metaphor for wings.

Sing.
    Sing.
Everything in balance and
better from above,
and life is applause that echoes
in the plane's throbbing depths.

Súbitamente
el corazón
voltea los panoramas inminentes;
todas las calles salen hacia la soledad de los horarios;
subversión
de las perspectivas evidentes;
looping the loop
en el trampolín romántico del cielo,
ejercicio moderno
en el ambiente ingenuo del poema;
la Naturaleza subiendo
el color del firmamento.

Al llegar te entregaré este viaje de sorpresas,
equilibrio perfecto de mi vuelo astronómico;
tú estarás esperándome en el manicomio de la tarde,
así, desvanecida de distancias,
acaso lloras sobre la palabra otoño.

Ciudades del norte
        de la América nuestra,
tuya y mía;

    New-York,
    Chicago,
    Baltimore.

Reglamenta el gobierno los colores del día,
puertos tropicales
del Atlántico,
azules litorales
del jardín oceanográfico,
donde se hacen señales
los vapores mercantes;
palmeras emigrantes,
río caníbal de la moda,
primavera, siempre tú, tan esbelta de flores.

Suddenly
the heart
flips imminent scenes;
all streets fall toward a scheduled solitude;
subversion
of evident perspectives;
looping the loop
on the sky's romantic springboard,
modern exercise
in the poem's naïve atmosphere;
Nature climbing
firmament's color.

I'll bring this voyage of surprises when I come,
my astronomical flight's perfect balance;
you'll wait for me in the madhouse afternoon,
like that, vanished in the distance,
maybe you weep over the word autumn.

Northern cities
          of our America,
yours and mine;

          New York,
          Chicago,
          Baltimore.

Government regulates day's colors,
tropical
Atlantic ports,
oceanographic garden
coastal blues,
where merchant steamships
signal;
emigrant palm trees,
fashionable cannibal river,
spring, always you, so slender in flowers.

País donde los pájaros hicieron sus columpios.
Hojeando tu perfume se marchitan las cosas,
y tú lejanamente sonríes y destellas,
¡oh novia electoral, carrusel de miradas!
lanzaré la candidatura de tu amor
hoy que todo se apoya en tu garganta,
la orquesta del viento y los colores desnudos.
Algo está aconteciendo allá en el corazón.

Las estaciones girando
mientras capitalizo tu nostalgia,
y todo equivocado de sueños y de imágenes;
la victoria alumbra mis sentidos
y laten los signos del zodíaco.

Soledad apretada contra el pecho infinito.
De este lado del tiempo,
sostengo el pulso de mi canto;
tu recuerdo se agranda como un remordimiento,
y el paisaje entreabierto se me cae de las manos.

Country where birds make their own swings.
Leaf through your perfume, things wither,
and you smile distant and sparkle,
oh electoral lover, carousel of gazes!
I launch my candidacy for your love
now that everything rests in your throat,
wind orchestra and naked colors.
Something's happening in my heart.

Seasons spin
while I fund your nostalgia
and every mistaken dream and image;
victory lights my senses
and zodiacal signs throb.

Solitude pressed against infinite breast.
From this side of time,
I sustain the song's pulse;
your memory grows as regret,
half-open, the landscape falls from my hands.

T.S.H.

Sobre el despeñadero nocturno del silencio
las estrellas arrojan sus programas,
y en el audión inverso del ensueño,
se pierden las palabras
olvidadas.

    T.S.H.
    de los pasos
    hundidos
    en la sombra
    vacía de los jardines.

El reloj
de la luna mercurial
ha ladrado la hora a los cuatro horizontes.

    La soledad
    es un balcón
    abierto hacia la noche.

¿En dónde estará el nido
de esta canción mecánica?

Las antenas insomnes del recuerdo
recogen ls mensajes
inalámbricos
de algún adiós deshilachado.

    Mujeres naufragadas
que equivocaron las direcciones
trasatlánticas;
y las voces

Wireless telegraphy

Stars cast programs
over nocturnal silence cliff,
in dream audion tubes
forgotten words
are lost.

    Wireless telegraphy
    of steps
    sunk
    in empty
    garden shadow.

Mercurial moon
clock
barks the hour to the four horizons.

    Solitude
    is a balcony
    open to night.

Where could this mechanical
song's nest be?

Memory's insomniac antennas
wirelessly
pick up some frayed
farewell signal.

    Shipwrecked women
who got wrong
transatlantic directions;
and voices

de auxilio
como flores
estallan en los hilos
de los pentagramas
internacionales.

El corazón
me ahoga en la distancia.

Ahora es el "Jazz-Band"
de Nueva York;
son los puertos sincrónicos
florecidos de vicio
y la propulsión de los motores.

Manicomio de Hertz, de Marconi, de Edison!

El cerebro fonético baraja
la perspectiva accidental
de los idiomas.
Hallo!

Una estrella de oro
ha caído en el mar.

of help
burst open like
flowers on sheet music
for international
anthems.

My heart
drowns me in distance.

Now is a New York
jazz band;
synchronous ports are
in flower with vice
and motor propulsion.

Madhouse of Hertz, Marconi, Edison!

Brain phonetic shuffles
languages, accidental
perspective.
¡Hola!

A gold star
falls in the sea.

Primavera

El jardín alusivo se envaguece de esperas
y el corazón despierta a las últimas cosas.

Un soplo de radiolas
avienta hacia nosotros
sus rumores de vidrio.

Los poetas comentan la renuncia del día.

Las calles vagabundas regresan del exilio.

Una tenue esperanza me llevó a sus caricias;
su imagen repentina me estremce en lo hondo;
anida su blancura en la tarde latente,
y mientras que desciñe su busto de suspiros
los árboles alumbran nuestro secreto cósmico.

La ausencia es el perfume que me deja en el pecho.
La pierdo en la espesura
de la vida moderna,
y nuevamente vuelvo
al campo de deportes con sus lunas auténticas.

Apuesto a su sonrisa en el juego de pokar,
lecturas de la música anegadas de lágrimas.

Cuando pongo en sus manos
el cheque de mi adiós,
los expresos sonámbulos
despiden nuestras sombras,
y el mare de los puertos dentro del corazón.

Spring

Allusive garden grows vague with hopes
and the heart wakes to last things.

Radiola puff
throws glass
rumors toward us.

Poets comment on the day's abdication.

Vagabond streets return from exile.

Faint hope carries me to her caresses;
her sudden image shakes me deep;
her whiteness nests in latent evening,
and while she unlaces her sighing bust
trees light our cosmic secret.

Absence is perfume left on my chest.
Lost in denseness
of modern life,
I go back once again,
to the ball field, its authentic moons.

I bet her smile in a poker game,
tear-flooded music recitals.

When I put a farewell
check in her hands,
sleepwalking expresses
took leave of our shadows,
and nausea in harbors of the heart.

(Solfea la primavera
sus lecciones.)

De pronto el desenlace obscuro de la célula.

Transaré con los pájaros su recuerdo sangrante.

(Spring do-re-mis
its lessons.)

Suddenly the cell's dark outcome.

I'll barter her bloody memory with birds.

80 H.P.

Pasan las avenidas del otoño
bajo los balcones marchitos de la música,
y el jardín es como un destello rojo
entre el aplauso burgués de las arquitecturas.

Esquinas flameadas de ponientes.

El automóvil sucinto
tiene a veces
ternuras
minerales.

Para la amiga interferente
entregada a las vueltas del peligro;

he aquí su sonrisa equilibrista,
sus cabellos boreales,
y sobre todo, el campo,
desparramado de caricias.

80 H.P.

Autumn avenues pass
under withered music balconies
and the garden a red sparkle
among architect's bourgeois applause.

Flaming sunset corners.

    The succinct automobile
    has at times
    mineral
    tenderness.

    For the meddling lady friend
    devoted to dangerous turns;

here her tightrope walker's smile
her northern hair
and above all, the caress-
scattered countryside.

Países del quitasol.

```
               nuevo
—espectáculo  mundo
exclusivo—            latino
           de sus ojos.
```

```
En el motor              ⎧  (El corazón apretado
hay la misma canción.    ⎩  como un puño)
```

A veces pasan ráfagas, paisajes estrujados,

y por momentos
el camino es angosto como un sueño.

Entre sus dedos
se deshoja
la rosa
de los vientos.

Los árboles turistas
a intervalos
regresan con la tarde.
Se van
quedando

atrás
los arrabales
del recuerdo

—oh el alegre motín de su blancura!—

Parasol countries

         her eyes'
—exclusive   new
spectacle—   latin
      world

The same song { (Heart tight
in the motor   as a fist)

Sometimes gusts, crumpled landscapes pass,

    and for a moment
    the road is dream narrow.

  Between her fingers
  the compass rose
    plucks
    its petals

  Tourist trees
  come back
  at intervals with evening.
  Ghettos

  of memory
  are left
  behind

    —oh the happy riot of her whiteness—

Tacubaya,   {   Pequeños
San Angel,   alrededores de la música.
Mixcoac.

Después
sólo las praderas   del tiempo

Allá lejos
   ejércitos
      de la noche
         nos esperan.

Tacubaya,   {   Small
San Angel,   suburbs of music.
Mixcoac.

Then
only meadows   of time

Further on
     armies
          of night
               await us.

Puerto

Llegaron nuestros pasos hasta la borda de la tarde;
el Atlántico canta debajo de los muelles
y presiento un reflejo de mujeres
que sonríen al comercio
de los países nuevos.

El humo de los barcos
desmadeja el paisaje;
brumosa a travesía
florecida de pipas.
¡Oh rubia transeúnte de las zonas marítimas,
de pronto eres la imagen
movible del acuario!

Hay un tráfico ardiente de avenidas
frente al hotel abanicado de palmeras.

Te asomas por la celosía
de las canciones
al puerto palpitante de motores
y los colores de la lejanía
me miran en tus tiernos ojos.

Entre las enredaderas venenosas
que enmarañan el sueño
recojo sus señales amorosas;
la dicha nos espera
en el alegre verano de sus besos;
la arrodilla el océano de caricias,
y el piano
es una hamaca en la alameda.

Port

Our steps arrive on evening's deck;
the Atlantic sings under piers,
my premonition: a reflection of women
who smile at commerce
in new countries.

Boat smoke
exhausts the landscape;
misty crossing
in flower with pipes,
oh blond sea traveler!
suddenly, you, the movable
aquarium image.

Ardent avenue traffic
before the palm-fanned hotel.

You show yourself
through song lattice
to the motor-throbbed port
and remote colors
watch me in your tender eyes.

I pick up amorous signals
among poison creeper
tangled around a dream;
joy awaits
in the happy summer of her kisses;
she makes the caress ocean kneel;
and the piano
is a boulevard hammock.

Se reúne la luna allá en los mástiles,
y un viento de ceniza
me arrebata tu nombre;
la navegación agitada de pañuelos
y los adioses surcan nuestros pechos,
y en la débil memoria de todos estos goces
sólo los pétalos de sus estremecimientos
perfuman las orillas de la noche.

The moon, met there on the masts,
and ash wind
snatches away her name;
agitated handkerchief navigation
and goodbyes cut furrows in our breasts,
and in faint memory of these pleasures,
only petals of her trembling
perfume shores of night.

Revolución

El viento es apóstol de esta hora interdicta.
Oh épocas marchitas
que sacudieron sus últimos otoños!
Barrunta su recuerdo los horizontes próximos
desahuciados de pájaros,
y las corolas deshojan se teclado.

Sopla el viento absoluto contra la materia
cósmica; la música
es la propaganda que flota en los balcones,
y el paisaje despunta
en las veletas.

Viento, dictadura
de hierro
que estremece las confederaciones!
Oh las muchedumbres
azules
y sonoras, que suben
hasta los corazones!

La tarde es un motín sangriento
en los suburbios;
árboles harapientos
que piden limosna en las ventanas;
las fábricas se abrasan
en el incendio de crepúsculo,
y en el cielo brillante
los aviones
ejecutan maniobras versperales.

Revolution

Wind, apostle of this prohibited hour.
Oh withered epochs,
shaken by final autumns!
Memory predicts the next
bird-evicted horizons,
and flowers pluck keyboard petals.

Absolute wind blows against cosmic
matter; music,
propaganda that floats on balconies,
and the landscape
abounds in weather vanes.

Wind, dictatorship
of iron,
shakes confederations!
Oh loud
blue
crowds that lift
our hearts!

Evening a bloody mutiny
in suburbs;
ragged trees
beg alms in windows;
factories burn
in fire of twilight,
and airplanes
execute dusk maneuvers
in bright sky.

Banderas clamorosas
repetirán su arenga proletaria
frente a las ciudades.

En el mitin romántico de la partida,
donde todos lloramos
hoy recojo la espera de su cita;
la estación
despedazada se queda entre sus manos,
y su desmayo
el el alto momento del adiós.
Beso la fotografía de su memoria
y el tren despavorido se aleja entre la sombra,
mientras deshojo los caminos nuevos.

Pronto llegaremos a la cordillera.
Oh tierna geografía
de nuestro México,
sus paisajes aviónicos,
alturas inefables de la economía
política; el humo de las factorías
perdidas en la niebla
del tiempo,
y los rumores eclécticos
de los levantamientos.
Noche adentro
los soldados,
se arrancaron
del pecho
las canciones populares.

La artillería
enemiga, nos espía
en las márgenes de la Naturaleza;
los ruidos subterráneos
pueblan nuestro sobresalto
y se derrumba el panorama.

Resounding flags
will echo the proletarian harangue
outside cities.

At the party's romantic rally,
where we all weep,
I harvest hope of seeing her;
the station
falls to pieces in her hands,
her fainting is
farewell's high point.
I kiss her memory's photograph
and the terrified train moves away through shadow,
while I pluck petals from new paths.

Soon we'll come to the mountains.
Oh tender geography
of our Mexico,
its airplane landscapes,
ineffable heights of political
economy; factory smoke
lost in mists
of time,
and electric rumors
of uprisings.
Dark within,
soldiers
tore
peoples' anthems
from their breasts.

The enemy
artillery eyes us
on Nature's margins;
subterranean noises
populate our fear
and the scene collapses.

Trenes militares
que van hacia los cuatro puntos cardinales,

al bautizo de sangre
donde todo es confusión,
y los hombres borrachos
juegan a los naipes
y a los sacrificios humanos;
trenes sonoros y marciales
donde hicimos cantando la Revolución.

Nunca como ahora me he sentido tan cerca de la muerte.
Pasamos la velada junto a la lumbre intacta del recuerdo
pero llegan los otros de improviso
apagando el concepto de las cosas,
las imágenes tiernas al borde del horóscopo.

Allá lejos,
mujeres preñadas
se han quedado rogando
por nosotros
a los Cristos de Piedra.

Después de la matanza
otra vez el viento
espanta
la hojarasca de los sueños.

Sacudo el alba de mis versos
sobre los corazones enemigos,
y el tacto helado de los siglos
me acaricia en la frente,
mientras que la angustia del silencio
corre por las entrañas de los nombres queridos.

Military trains
head for four cardinal points,

to baptism in blood
where all is confusion,
and drunk men
play at cards
and human sacrifice,
loud martial trains
where, singing, we make Revolution.

I've never felt so close to death as now.
We pass the night beside memory's intact fire
but others come unexpectedly
snuff out concepts of things,
tender images on horoscope's edge.

Out there,
pregnant women
go on praying
to stone Christs
for us.

After the slaughter
wind again
frightens away
fallen dream leaves.

I shake dawn from my verses
over enemy hearts,
the frozen touch of centuries
strokes my forehead,
while anguish of silence
runs through guts beloved of name.

Partida

Yo soy una estación sentimental
y los adioses pitan como trenes.
Es inútil llorar.

En los contornos del crepúsculo,
ventanas encendidas
hacia los rumbos
nuevos.

Palpita
todavía
    la alondra
       vesperal
          de su pañuelo.

Departure

I'm a sentimental station
and goodbyes whistle like trains.
It's useless to cry.

In twilight outlines
windows lit
toward new
directions,

Still
shaking
   handkerchief
      dusk
         lark.

Ruta

A bordo del expreso
volamos sobre la irrealidad del continente.

La tarde apagada en los espejos,
y los adioses sangran en mi mente.

El corazón nostálgico presiente
a lo largo de este viaje,
literaturas vagabundas
que sacudieron las plumas
de sus alas,
en los fríos corredores del paisaje.

Van pasando las campiñas sonámbulas
mientras el tren se aleja entre los túneles del sueño.

Allá de tarde en tarde,
ciudades
apedreadas de gritos y adioses.

Ríos de adormideras
que viened del fondo de los años,
pasan interminablemente,
bajo los puentes,
que afirmaron su salto metálico
sobre las vertientes.

Después, montañas, silenciosos ejércitos
aullan la muerte.

Route

On board the express
we fly over continental unreality.

Evening dulled in mirrors,
farewells bleed in my mind.

My nostalgic heart predicts
vagabond literatures
that shook feathers
from wings,
in landscape's cold corridors
along this journey.

Sleepwalking countrysides pass
while the train distances dream tunnels.

There, sometimes,
cities
stoned by farewell shouts.

Rivers of poppies
from depths of years,
pass without end
beneath bridges,
those affirmed
metallic leaps
over slopes.

Then, mountains, silent armies
howl at death.

Entre las rendijas de la noche
me atormenta el insomnio de una estrella.
Trenes que marchan siempre hacia la ausencia,
un día,
sin saberlo,
nos cruzaremos
en la geografía.

A star's insomnia torments me
through cracks in the night.
Trains that always march toward absence,
one day,
without knowing it,
we'll cross paths
on that geography.

Paroxismo

Camino de otros sueños salimos con la tarde;
una extraña aventura
nos deshojó en la dicha de la carne,
y el corazón fluctúa
entre ella y la desolación del viaje.

En la aglomeración de los andenes
rompieron de pronto los sollozos;
después, toda la noche
debajo de mis sueños,
escucho sus lamentos
y sus ruegos.

El tren es una ráfaga de hierro
que azota el panorama y lo conmueve todo.

Apuro su recuerdo
hasta el fondo
del éxtasis,
y laten en el pecho
los colores lejanos de sus ojos.

Hoy pasaremos junto del otoño
y estarán amarillas las praderas.

¡Me estremezco por ella!
¡Horizontes deshabitados de la ausencia!

Mañana estará todo
nublado de sus lágrimas
y la vida que llega
es débil como un soplo.

Paroxysm

Path of other dreams we leave with evening;
strange adventure
strips our leaves in joy of flesh
and my heart fluctuates
between her and journey's desolation.

In station platform crowds
sobs suddenly erupt;
then, all night
beneath my dreams,
I listen to their laments,
their prayers.

The train is an iron gust
that roams the landscape, moving everything.

I exhaust her memory
to the ends
of ecstasy,
and her eyes' distant colors
beat in my chest.

Today we'll pass beside autumn
and the meadows will be yellow.

I tremble for her!
Horizons emptied of absence!

Tomorrow all will be
darkened by her tears
and the coming life
is faint as breeze.

Evocación

Al final de este viaje
he inclinado mis sueños
sobre la barandilla de su nombre.

El agua turbia de la sombra
ha metido la noche
hasta los corazones.

—Muchedumbres inmóviles
están asediando el horizonte.—

He apretado su imagen
contra mi desconsuelo,
y la luna, apoyada en los cristales,
es el frío
deshielo
de su frente.

Un perfume imprevisto
la enciende en mi memoria;
tiene el "filing" latino
su actitud de dulzura.
Oh su carne platónica,
inocente
geometría que descansa en su seno!

La sonrisa es la flor del equilibrio orgánico,
y el campo
la estremece,
bajo mi abrazo
panorámico.

Evocation

At journey's end
I've draped dreams
over the banister of her name.

Night has put
even our hearts
in shadow's muddy water.

   —Immobile crowds
   smoothe the horizon.—

I've clutched her image
against my grief,
and the moon, leaning against windows,
is her brow's
thawing
cold.

An unexpected perfume
ignites her in memory;
she has a Latin "feeling"
a pose of sweetness.
Oh Platonic flesh,
innocent
geometry that rests in her breast!

Her smile the flower of organic balance,
and the land
shakes her,
under my panoramic
embrace.

Pero a pesar de todo,
el otoño
inquilino
regó de hojas secas su recuerdo.

Oh mi novia lejana,
humareda romántica
de los primeros versos.

But despite everything,
autumn,
that lodger,
begs her memory from fallen leaves.

Oh distant lover,
romantic smoke
of my first poems.

Saudade

Estoy solo en el último tramo de la ausencia
y el dolor hace horizonte en mi demencia.

Allá lejos,
el panorama maldito.

¡Yo abandoné la Confederación sonora de su carne!

Sore todo su voz,
hecha pedazos
entre los tubos
de la música!

En el jardín interdicto
  —azoro unánime—
el auditorio congelado de la luna.

Su recuerdo es sólo una resonancia
entre la arquitectura del insomnio.

¡Dios mío,
tengo las manos llenas de sangre!

Y los aviones,
pájaros de estos climas estéticos,
no escribirán su nombre
en el agua del cielo.

Saudade

Alone in the last land of absence,
and pain makes a horizon in my dementia.

Out there,
the damned landscape.

I left the sonorous Confederation of flesh!

Above all her voice,
worn out
through tubes
of music!

In forbidden garden
        —unanimous alarm—
frozen audience of the moon.

Her memory is but an echo
through architecture of insomnia.

My God,
the blood on my hands!

And airplanes,
birds of aesthetic climate,
will not write her name
in water of sky.

APPENDIX:

THE FIRST STRIDENTIST

MANIFESTO

1921

ACTUAL - N°1

Hoja de Vanguardia

Comprimido Estridentista de Manuel Maples Arce

Iluminaciones Subversivas de Renée Dunan, F. T. Marinetti, Guillermo de Torre, Lasso de la Vega, Salvat-Papasseit, etc., y Algunas Cristalizaciones Marginales.

E MUERA EL CURA HIDALGO
X ABAJO SAN-RAFAEL-SAN
I LAZARO
T ESQUINA
O SE PROHIBE FIJAR ANUNCIOS

I.— EN nombre de la vanguardia actualista de México, sinceramente interesado de todas las pigmas notariales y cédulas consagradas al sistema cartulario, con veinte siglos de éxito efímero en farmacias y droguerías subvencionadas por la ley, me en el vértice eclatante de mi insustituible categoría presentista, equilibrándome en el asintológicamente revolucionario, telarines con todo el mundo. Afuera de eje, se concentra estridentemente en torno de las manos tendidas, insurrecto y categóricamente afirmo, sin más excepciones a los "players" diametralmente explosivos en inmediatos fotográficos y gritos acorralados, que mi actitud: último fusilando y acordado para defenderme de las películas literales de los últimos pseudoantis intelectivos: Muera el Cura Hidalgo, Abajo San Rafael, San Lázaro, Esquina. Se prohibe fijar anuncios.

Mi locura no está en los presupuestos. La verdad, no acontece ni sucede nunca fuera de nosotros. La vida es sólo un método sin puertas que se llueve a intervalos. De aquí que insista en la literatura insuperable en que se prestigian los teléfonos y diálogos perfumados que se hibridan al despeje por hilos conductoras. La verdad estética, es tan sólo un estado de emoción incolorable desarrollado en plano estraslegal de equivalencia integralista. Las cosas no tienen valor intrínseco posible, y su equivalencia poética, florece en sus relaciones y cordinaciones; las que sólo se manifiestan en un sector interno, más emocionante y más escultórico que una realidad desmantelada, puede verse en fragmento de una de mis anticipaciones poemáticas novaltástolicas): "Esas Rosas Eléctricas..." (Cosmópolis.—No. 34). Para hacer una obra de arte, como dice Pierre Albert-Birot, es preciso crear, y no copiar. "Nuestros horizontes la verdad en la realidad parece, y en la realidad aparente". En este instante asistimos al espectáculo de nosotros mismos. Todo debe ser superación y equivalencia en nuestros iluminados panoramas a que nos circunscriben los esféricos cínicos actualistas, pues pienso con Epstein, que no debemos limitar a la Naturaleza, sino estudiar sus leyes, y comportarnos en el fondo como ella.

II.— Toda técnica de arte, está destinada a llenar una función espiritual en un momento determinado. Cuando los medios expresionistas son inhábiles e insuficientes para traducir nuestras emociones personales,—única y elemental finalidad estética,—es necesario, y esto contra toda la fuerza estacionaria y afraccionaria localizarnos de la crítica oficial, emplear la corriente y desnudar los "switchs". Una pechera reumática se ha carbonizado, pero no por esto he de abandonar el juego, ¿Quién se equivocó? Ahora el cubismo está en Cipriano Max-Jacob, y su sensacionalismo por la que respecta a aquel periodista circunsparto, mientras Blaise Cendrars, que siempre está en el plano de superación, no pierde el equilibrio, intencionalmente le equivocado, ignora, si sagrado que tiene abiertos los ojos en un cielo estrellado a una gota de agua al microscopio.

III.— "Un automóvil en movimiento, es más bello que la Victoria de Samotracia". A esta constante afirmación del vanguardista italiano Marinetti, exaltada por Lucini, Buzzi, Cavacchioli, etc., yuxtapongo mi apasionamiento decisivo por las máquinas de escribir, y mi amor efusivísimo por la literatura de los avisos económicos. Cuanta mayor, y más honda emoción he logrado vivir en un recorte de periódico arbitrario y sugerente, que en todos esos organilléricamente pseudo-líricos y bombones melódicos para recitales de chaparros grafía a las señoritas, declaracionistamente inferidos ante el auditorio distprintivo de niñas frac-troteantes y expansiones y burguesas temerosas por sus comadrinos y sus ciencias de escándalo como válentimente afirma mi hermano espiritual Guillermo de Torre, en su manifiesto yuxta ladó en la primera explosión ultrísta de Paritonia, y esto, sin perder toda esas geometrizaciones (sic) intuitivamente aplastadas en chalorladas literarias, en que sólo se justifica el reflejo cartomario de algunos literaturiados "ajustente".

IV.— Es necesario exaltar en todos los tonos estridentes de nuestro diapasón propagandista, la belleza actualista de las máquinas, de los puentes gloriosamente cacareantes exclatidos sobre las vertientes por adoración al sexo, el humo de las fábricas, las emociones cubistas de los grandes trasatlánticos con humeantes chimeneas de ruin y negro, anclados hormológicamente—Ruiz Huidobro—junto a los muelles efervescentes congestionados, el régimen industrialista de las grandes ciudades palpitantes, las blusas azules de los obreros explosivos en esta hora emocionante y conmovida; toda esta belleza del siglo, tan fuertemente intuída por Emi-

lio Verhaeren, tan sinceramente amada por Nicolás Beauduin, y tan ampliamente significada y comprendida por todos los artistas de vanguardia. Al fin, los trenvías, han sido redimidos del dicterio de prosaicos, en que prestigiosamente se había valorizado la burguesía vestruída con hojas contadas por tantos años de retardatario sucesivo e intransigencia sustanciosa de archivos cronológicos.

V.— Chopin a la silla eléctrica! He aquí una afirmación higienista y deberosa. Ya los futuristas mal-adaptógrafos, pidieron en le traz de molde el asquroso del claro de luna, y los ultraístas españoles, tranterioas, por voz de Rafael Cansinos Assens, la liquidación de las hojas secas, realmente agitada en periódicos y hojas subversivas. Como ellos, es de urgencia telegráfica emplear un método radicalista y diletanta. Chopin a la silla eléctrica! (M. M. A. trade mark) es una preparación maravillosa; así vende y cuatro horas exterminta todos los gérmenes de la literatura petrificada y su equivalentemente, el mismo valor emocional que las tenía adorables de nuestras corralistas y exquisitas actualistas.

#

NOW

NUMBER 1

AVANT-GARDE BROADSIDE

MANUEL MAPLES ARCE'S

STRIDENTIST MANIFESTO

Subversive illustrations from Renée Dunan, F.T. Marinetti, Guillermo de Torre, Lasso de la Vega, Salvat Papasseit, etc., and a few marginal crystallizations.

S	DEATH TO FATHER HIDALGO
U	DOWN WITH SAINT RAPHAEL
CC	SAINT LAZARUS ▰▰▰▰▰
E	CORNER ▰▰▰▰▰
SS	POST NO BILLS ▰▰▰▰

In the name of the modern Mexican avant-garde, sincerely horrified by all the notarized plaques and signs consecrated by the chartulary system, with twenty centuries of effusive success in pharmacies and drugstores subsidized by the law, I centralize myself on the striking apex of my irreplaceable presentist category, equilaterally convinced and eminently revolutionary, while everyone off the axis watches astonished, wringing their hands, I affirm, imperatively and categorically, with no more exceptions made for the diametrically opposed "players" in photographic blazes and corralled screams, my pure, destructive Stridentism, to defend myself from the literal stones of the latest intellectual plebiscites: Death to Father Hidalgo, Down with San Rafael, San Lazaro, Corner: Post No Bills.

I.

My madness is not in presuppositions. Truth neither happens nor ever takes place outside of ourselves. Life is only a doorless method that rains from time to time. From here, it insists on an insuperable literature that honors telephones, perfumed dialogues joined carelessly together by conducting wires. Aesthetic truth is only a state of incoercible emotion developing on an extrabasal plane of integralist equivalence. Things have no possible intrinsic value, and their poetic equivalence flowers in their relations and coordinations, which manifest only in an internal sector, more exciting and more definitive than a dismantled reality, as can be seen in fragments of one of my poematic neolatitudinal anticipations: "Those Electric Roses..." (*Cosmopolis*, no. 34). To make a work of art, as Pierre Albert-Birot says, is precisely to create and not to copy. "We seek truth in thought reality, and not in apparent reality." At this moment, we watch the spectacle of ourselves. Everything must be overcoming and equivalence in our illuminated panoramas, circumscribed as we are by spherical modern skies, because I think, as does Epstein, that we must not imitate Nature, but study its laws and behave fundamentally as it does.

II.

Every artistic technique is destined to fulfill a spiritual function at a determined moment. When the means of expression are unable or insufficient to translate our personal emotions—the only and elemental aesthetic finality—it is necessary, and this against all the stationary force and philistine affirmations of official criticism, to cut off the current and break the switches. A rheumatic starched shirt has been carbonized, but that's no reason to abandon the game. Follow? Now the dice lands on Cipriano Max-Jacob and that circumspect journalist is respected for sensationalism, while Blaise Cendrars, who is always overcoming, without losing his balance, intentionally mistaken, doesn't know if what covers his eyes is a starry sky or a microscoped water drop.

III.

"An automobile in motion is more beautiful than the Victory of Samothrace." To this striking affirmation of the Italian avant-gardist Marinetti, exalted by Luccini, Buzzi, Cavacchioli, etcetera, I juxtapose my decisive passion for typewriters and my super effusive love for the literature of economic bulletins. How much more, and deeper, emotion have I managed to experience in an arbitrary, suggestive newspaper clipping than in all those psuedo-lyrical organgrinderisms and melodic bonbons, cowbell recitals free for young ladies, declamatorially deduced from the auditory disjunction of fox-trotted girls and spasmatics and bourgeois gentlemen afraid of their concubines and their strongboxes, as my spiritual brother Guillermo de Torre bravely affirms in his egoist manifesto, read at the first Parisian Ultraist explosion, and this, without perforating all these poemitzations (*sic*) enthusiastically applauded in literary chit-chats, in which alone the cardboard reflection of those pedestrialiterary "specimens" is justified.

IV.

It is necessary to exalt, in all the Stridentist tones of our propagandistic tuning fork, the modern beauty of machines, of gymnast bridges strongly stretched over slopes by concrete muscles, the smoke of factories, the cubist emotions of great transatlantic ships with smoking red and black chimneys, horoscopically anchored —Ruiz Huidobro— beside the effervescent, congested piers, the industrial regime of great palpitating cities, the blue shirts of explosive workers in this moving and exciting moment; all the beauty of this century, so strongly intuited by Emilio Verhaeren, so sincerely loved by Nicolás Beauduin and so amply dignified and understood by all the artists of the avant-garde. Finally, streetcars have been left out of the directory of prosaicisms which has, for so many years of successive delay and the melancholic intransigence of chronological archives, prestigiously valorized the big-bellied bourgeoisie with marriageable daughters.

V.

Chopin to the electric chair! A cleansing, hygienic affirmation. Anti-selenographic futurists already demanded, in moldy letters, the murder of moonlight, and the Spanish Ultraists transcribed, with the voice of Rafael Cansinos Assens, the liquidation of dry leaves recently agitated in magazines and subversive broadsides. Like them, it's telegraphically urgent to employ an efficient, radical method. Chopin to the electric chair (trademark M.M.A.) is a marvelous preparation; in twenty-four hours it exterminates all the germs of a putrefied literature and its use is so very agreeable and beneficial. Shake well before using. We commit our crime against the outdated melancholism of the "Nocturnes" and we proclaim, synchronically, the aristocracy of gasoline. The blue smoke of exhaust pipes, which smells of modernity and dynamism has, equivalently, the same emotional value as our correlative and exquisite avant-gardist's adorable veins.

VI.

Provincial wallets iron souvenir streetcar tickets flat. Where is the Hotel Iturbide? All the dyspeptic newspapers have indigestion from stereotypes of María Conesa, intermittently on the front page, and there's even some who dare to be integrally amazed over the National Theater's architectonic alarm, but there hasn't been anyone, yet, susceptible to liminal emotions on the margin of that automotive place, mended with stupendous posters and geometric signs. Smooth vats: blues, yellows, reds. In half a glass of gasoline we have literally drank Avenida Juárez, 80 horses. I tilt myself on the prolonging of an improvised ellipse, forgetting the statue of Carlos IV. Automobile accessories, Haynes replacement parts, accumulating and dynamic tires, chassis, brakes, klaxon horns, spark plugs, lubricants, gasoline. I'm mistaken. Moctezuma de Orizaba is the best beer in Mexico, smoke Buen Tono, S.A. cigars, etcetera, etcetera. A perpendicular brick has run aground on those schematic scaffolds. Everything trembles. My sensations amplify. The penultimate facade falls on me.

VII.

No more creationism, dadaism, paroxysm, expressionism, synthesism, imagism, suprematism, cubism, orpheism, etcetera, "isms" more or less theorized and efficient. We make a quintessential and purifying synthesis of all flowering tendencies on the maximal plane of our modern, illuminated exaltation, not from a false conciliatory desire, —synthesism—, but from a rigorous aesthetic conviction and spiritual urgency. It's not a matter of gathering up prismal methods, basically anti-seismic, so as to ferment them, mistakenly, in glasses of fraternal etiquette, but intrinsically organic tendencies, of easy reciprocal adaptation which, resolving all the equations of the modern technical problem, so sinuous and complicated, illuminates our marvelous desire to totalize the inner emotions and sensorial suggestions in a multitudinous and polyhedral form.

VIII.

Humanity is not a leveled out, systematic watch mechanism. Sincere emotion is a form of supreme arbitrariness and specific disorder. Everyone attempts the system of a well-regulated amateur band, of fixing their ideas, presenting a single aspect of the emotion, which is original and three-dimensionally spherical, with sincerist pretexts of primarily dominant clarity and simplicity, forgetting that in whatever panoramic moment this manifests, through nothing more than elemental, conscious terms, but also by a strong binary projection of inner movements, torpidly sensible to external means, but on the other hand, prodigiously reactive to the roto-translatory propulsions of the ideal plane of aesthetic truth that Apollinaire called the golden section. From here, there exists a broader interpretation of the electrolyzed personal emotions in the positive of the new technical procedures, because these crystallize a unanimous, totalizing aspect of life. Ideas often derail themselves, and are never continuous and successive, but simultaneous and intermittent. (II. *Profond aujour d'hui*, Cendrars, Cosmopolis, num. 33). In a single canvas, dioramically, they fix and superimpose themselves rigorously coinciding on the vertex of the introspective instant.

IX.

And sincerity? Who's asking? One moment, gentlemen, while we change coals. All eyes have negated themselves with aluminum, and that distracted lady walks superficially over lateral advertisements. A graphic demonstration. In the living room they have intermittent dialogues, and a friend is resolute on the keyboard. The electric chrysanthemum plucks its petals on mercurial heights. But that isn't all. The neighbors burn gasoline as incense. In the tabloids there are ministerial stupidities. My abstracted fingers are diluted in the smoke. And now, I ask, who is more sincere? We who do not tolerate strange influences, who purify and crystallize ourselves in the synesthesic filter of our most personal emotions, or all those chloro-ideologically diurnalist "powers" who try only to ingratiate themselves with the amorous masses of an insufficient, dictatorial, mentally incapacitated public of officious cretins, academic photophobes and strikebreaking traffickers and plenaries?

X.

Let us cosmopolitanize ourselves. It's no longer possible to keep ourselves in the conventional confines of national art. The news expends itself by telegraph, over the skyscrapers, those marvelous skyscrapers so vituperated by everyone, there are dromedary clouds and, among their knitted muscles, the electric elevator moves. Forty-eighth floor. One, two, three, four, etcetera. We've arrived. And over a gymnast's parallel bars in the open air, locomotives swallow kilometers. Steam that smokes toward absence. Everything approaches and goes away in the moving moment. The means change and their influence changes everything. Of cultural and genetic approximations, profiles and racial characteristics tend to be erased by means of an eminently selective, rigorous labor, while modern meridians, the psychological unity of the century, flower in the sun. The only frontiers possible in art are the impassible ones of our marginalist emotion.

XI.

To fix the aesthetic limits. To make art, with its own congenital elements fertilized in its own environment. Not to reintegrate values, but to totally create them and, at the same time, to destroy all the mistakenly modern theories, false because interpretative, such as the impressionist derivation (post-impressionism) and luminist suffixes (divisionism, vibrationism, pointillism, etcetera). To make pure poetry, suppressing every strange and denatured element (description, anecdote, perspective). To suppress, in painting, every mental suggestion and false literaturism, so applauded by our buffoonish critics. To set limits, not in Lessing's interpretive parallel but in the place of overcoming and equivalence. A new art, as Reverdy affirms, requires a new syntax, Braque's assertion being here positive: the painter thinks in colors, I deduce the need for a new colorist syntax.

XII.

No retrospection. No futurism. The whole world, there, quiet, marvelously illuminated on the stupendous axis of the present moment; observed in the prodigy of its unique, unmistakable emotion and sensorially electrolyzed on the suprematist "I," vertical over the meridian instant, always the same and always new. We make nowism. Walter Conrad Arensberg exalts in the affirmative stridency that ensures that his poems will live for only six hours; and we love our unconquered century. You say the public lacks the intellectual resources to penetrate our formidable, dynamic aesthetic? Very good. Let them stay in the lobby or resign themselves to vaudeville. Our egoism is now superlative; our conviction, unbreakable.

XIII.

It pleases me to take part in the numerous phonographic clientele of my potential stylists, bilious critics in rags, chewed by all the lacerating ulcers of the old stinking, agonizing literature, specifically obtuse and slow-witted academics, traditionally ignorant and every type of exoteric android, prodigiously successful in our rigorous, reeking intellectual climate, with which they surely prepare my perspective skies, which are on every point useless, their stingy angers and ridiculous operetta bragging, since in my integral radicalist, extremist conviction, in my unpublished isolation and my glorious intransigence, they will find only the electrifying hermeticism of my negating, subversive laugh. What spiritual relation, what ideological affinity, can exist between that Mr. who has dressed himself in a tailcoat to wash dishes and the music of Erik Satie? With that gilded word: Stridentism, I transcribe the Dada signs, which are made of nothing, to combat the "official nothing of books, exhibitions and theater." In synthesis a radical force opposed against the caring conservatism of a collective annihilation.

XIV.

Success to all the young poets, painters and sculptors of Mexico, to those who haven't been ruined yet by by the perks of government sinecures, to those who have not been corrupted by the tight-fisted elegies of official criticism and the applause of a rude, lustful public, to all those who haven't gone to lick the plates at Enrique González Martínez's culinary banquets, to make art (!) with the stylicide of their intellectual menstruations, to all the great sincere, to those who haven't decomposed in the lamentable, foul-smelling efflorescence of our nationalist atmosphere with the stench of pulque and embers of fried food, to all those, success in the name of the modern avant-garde of Mexico, that they may come and fight at our side in the luciferian ranks of the "decouvert," where, I say with Lasso de la Vega: "We are far from the spirit of beasts. Like Zarathustra we have freed ourselves from the weight, we have shaken off our prejudices. Our grand laughter is grand laughter. And here we are writing on new tablets." To finish up, I ask for the heads of the scholastic nightingales who make poetry into a simple rhapsodian can-can, raised on the slats of a chair: plucked after the rainstorm in the councilman's corrals of a bourgeois Sunday. Logic is an error and the right to wholeness is a monstrous joke, which interrupts the intelligencesticide Renée Durnan, Salvat-Papasseit, falling from a swing, has read this announcement on the screen: spit on the bald heads of cretins, and while the whole world, which remains off its axis, contemplates themselves spherically astonished, wringing their hands, I, gloriously alone, illuminate myself in the marvelous incandescence of my electric nerves.

AVANT-GARDE DIRECTORY

Rafael Cansinos Assens. Ramón Gómez de la Serna. Rafael Lasso de la Vega. Guillermo de Torre. Jorge Luis Borges. Cleotilde Luisi. Vicente Ruiz Huidobro. Gerardo Diego. Eugenio Montes. Pedro Garfias. Lucía Sánchez Saornil. J. Rivas Panedas. Ernesto López Parra. Juan Larrea. Joaquín de la Escosura. José de Cma y Escalante. César A. Comet. Isac del Vando Villar. Adriano del Valle. Juan Las. Mauricio Bacarisse. Rogelio Buendía. Vicente Risco. Pedro Raida. Antonio Espina. Adolfo Salazar. Miguel Romero Martínez. Ciriquiain Caitarro. Antonio M. Cubero. Joaquín Edwards. Pedro Iglesias. Joaquín de Aroca. León Felipe. Eliodoro Puche. Prieto Romero. Correa Calderón.

Francisco Vighi. Hugo Mayo. Bartolomé Galíndez. Juan Ramón Jiménez. Ramon del Valle Inclán. José Ortega y Gasset. Alfonso Reyes. José Juan Tablada. Diego M. Rivera. D. Alfaro Siqueiros. Mario de Zayas. José D. Frías. Fermín Revueltas. Silvestre Revueltas. P. Echevarría. Atl. J. Torres García. Rafael P. Barradas. J. Salvat. Papasseit. José María Yenoy. Jean Epstein. Jean Richard Bloch. Pierre Brune. Marie Blanchard. Corneau. Farrey. Fournier. Riou. Mme. Ghy Lohem. Marie Laurencin. Dunozer de Segonzac. Honneger. Georges Auric. Ozenfant. Alberto Gleizes. Pierre Reverdy. Juan Gris. Nicolás Beauduin. William Speth. Jean Paulhan. Guillermo Apollinaire. Cypien. Max. Jacob. Jorge Braque. Survage. Coris. Tritst Tzara. Francisco Picabia. Jorge Ribemont. Dessaigne. Renée Dunan. Archipenko. Soupault. Bretón. Paul Elouard. Marcel Duchamp. Frankel. Sernen. Erik Satie. Elie Faure. Pablo Picasso. Walter Bonrad Arensberg. Celine Arnauld. Walter Pach. Bruce. Morgan Roussel. Marc Chagall. Herr Baader. Max Ernst. Christian Schaad. Lipchitz. Ortíz de Zárate. Correia d'Araujo. Jacobsen. Schkold. Adam Fischer. Mme. Fischer. Peer Kroogh. Alf Rolfsen. Jeauneiet. Piet Mondrian. Torstenson. Mme. Alika. Ostrom. Geline. Salto. Weber. Wuster. Kokodika. Kandinsky. Steremberg (Com. de B.A. de Moscou). Mme. Lunacharsky. Erhenbourg. Taline. Konchalowsy. Machkoff. Mme. Ekster. Wlle Monate. Marewna. Larionow. Gondiarowa. Belova. Sontine. Daiibler. Doesburg. Raynal. Zahn. Derain. Walterowua Zur = Mueklen. Jean Cocteau. Pierre Albert. Birot. Metsinger. Jean Charlot. Maurice Reynal Pieux. F.T. Marinetti. G.P. Lucinni. Paolo Buzzi. A. Palazzeschi. Enrique Cavacchioli. Libero Altomare. Luciano Folgore. E. Cardile. G. Carrieri. E. Mansella Fontini. Auro d'Alba. Mario Betuda. Armando Mazza. M. Boccioni. C.D. Carrá. G. Severini. Ballila Pratella. Cangiullo. Corra. Mariano. Boccini. Fessy. Setimelli. Carli. Ochsé. Linati. Tita Rosa. Saint-Point. Divoire. Martini. Moretti. Pirandello. Tozzi. Evola.

Ardengo. Sarcinio. Tovolato. Daubler. Doesburg. Broglio. Utrillo. Fabri. Vatrignant. Liege. Norah Borges. Savory. Gimmi. Van Gogh. Grunewald. Derain. Cauconnet. Boussingautl. Marquet. Gernez. Fobeen. Delaunay. Kurk. Scchwiters. Heyniche. Klem. Zirner. Gino. Galli. Bottai. Cioccatto. George Bellows. Giorgio de Chirico. Modigliani. Cantarelli. Soficci. Carena. et cetera.

Notes to the Poems

With the exception of the manifesto, which was translated specifically for this volume, all these translations were made in 2009, at the same time as *CITY*, which appeared as an Ugly Duckling Presse chapbook in 2010. The target English was modernist in tone, though it should be noted that most high modernist poetry in English was not quite as linguistically intense as that in other languages. I've used a sort of paraphrase technique in places, and shifted word order around in lines, as well as lines in stanzas, to get the effect I was going for. That and a preference for the more dynamic word among several possibilities have helped capture something of Maples's voice, while evading the danger of giving the poems a more Romantic feel than they have in the original. —*KMC*

Inner Scaffolds

Osram's catalogue — Osram was, and remains, a German manufacturer of lighting equipment. In the early 1920s they were particularly famous for their lightbulbs.

d'Orsay — As in Paris's Musée d'Orsay, which was the world's first electrified train station before it was a museum. The name is that of an aristocratic French family of prominent artists and collectors.

many-minded — The Spanish word that Maples uses, *multánime*, was the name of a café frequented by the Stridentists. Germán List Arzubide describes it as a "mechanical café where the waiters placed their orders via radio and the pianola played music from intercepted Martian concerts . . ."

Russia's lungs — This and further mentions of Russia's influence on Mexico are not references to Leon Trotsky, who did not arrive in Mexico until 1937, 13 years after this poem's publication.

Literary dick gropers — The gender of this noun in Maples's Spanish is male, leading some to label it a homophobic statement. And so it essentially is. The Stridentists' main poetic rivals, a group known as the Contemporaries, contained several prominent homosexuals, such as Xavier Villaurrutia. Though it should be noted that a Spanish noun referring to a mixed group automatically takes the male gender, while the term *asalta braguetas* (literally "attacker of trouser flies") is an insult aimed more at sexual appetite than orientation.

Obregonism — General Álvaro Obregón was a farmer-turned-general from the state of Sonora. As the Revolution in Mexico progressed, its leaders continually split into factions. Four allies would divide, two against two, and then the victors would again split and fight each other. Obregón was an ally of Venustiano Carranza, fighting and defeating Emiliano Zapata and Pancho Villa. Leading up to the 1920 election Obregón and Carranza split and Obregón launched what amounted to a second revolution, which he won. He held the presidency from 1920 to 1924, the period just prior to the writing of this poem.

the marathon night — The word here translated as "marathon" is *tarahumara*, the name of the Tarahumara Indian tribe, used as an adjective. The Tarahumara, native to what is today the Mexican state of Chihuahua, are world famous for their long distance running ability: see *Born to Run* by Christopher McDougall (Alfred A. Knopf, 2009).

Ocotlán — Small town in the Mexican state of Jalisco, site of the defeat of an armed insurrection against Obregón led by Adolfo de la Huerta, essentially the final major armed conflict of the Mexican Revolution.

Prohibited Poems

Wireless Telegraphy — The title of this poem in Spanish, "T.S.H.," is an archaic abbreviation for *telefonía sin hilos*, aka early radio, here rendered fully and literally into English. This poem was, appropriately, the first read over the radio in Mexico.

The First Stridentist Manifesto

Figures not noted here are either well-known enough to not require it or, in some cases, unidentifiable.

Cosmopolis — Spanish avant-garde journal aligned with Creationism/Ultraism, published from 1919 until 1922, in which many leading Spanish-language writers published, including Borges and Maples Arce.

Pierre Albert-Birot (1876-1967) — French poet, impresario, and editor, and a close friend of Apollinaire. Published many major avant-garde writers in his journal *SIC*.

Guillermo de Torre (1900-1971) — Spanish essayist and poet, author of the Ultraist manifesto, collaborator of Tristan Tzara and Borges, his brother-in-law.

Emilio Verhaeren (1855-1916) — Émile Verhaeren. Belgian symbolist poet and critic, frequent nominee for the Nobel Prize.

Nicolas Beauduin (1880-1960) — Apparently untranslated French poet, associated with a movement known as Paroxyism.

Rafael Cansinos Assens (1882-1964) — Prolific translator and poet from Spain, a major early influence on Borges and the Spanish avant-garde in general.

María Conesa (1892-1978) — AKA La Gatita Blana (The White Kitten). Spanish-born vaudeville actress of the revolutionary period who went on to a film and television career.

Walter Conrad Arensberg (1878-1954) — Famous now mostly for his art collection, he was also a poet and critic. He and his wife hosted a regular salon at their New York apartment, attended by Marcel Duchamp, Mina Loy, Man Ray, William Carlos Williams, and many others.

Salvat-Papasseit (1894-1924) — First name Joan. Catalan avant-garde poet.

The Avant-Garde Directory — We reproduce Maples Arce's list following Luis Mario Schneider's anthology, *Estridentismo: Una literatura de estrategia* (Insituto Nacional de Bellas Artes, 1970), and retain the original's romanizations, idiosyncratic abbreviations, and spellings. Detailed biographies of all the figures mentioned here would be beyond the scope of the present volume.

Translator's Note

Translation projects like this one, involving explicitly communist political art, are difficult. Often it is not possible to publish them at all, as evidenced by how little of an excellent poet like Roque Dalton's work has made it into English. When it is possible to publish, the conversation around the work can take on overtones of "recovering" what was "lost." This kind of conversation has the same problems of the passive voice as headlines about police shootings. And for the same reasons. Because the truth of the matter is that literature of this kind, especially from Latin America, was not lost. It was murdered, hidden, erased.

In Stridentism's case, some of that erasure was done by Maples himself, but this has to be considered in the context of post-revolutionary Mexican politics. Especially relevant here is the rise of the Institutional Revolutionary Party (PRI), which came to power just after Stridentism collapsed and controlled Mexico for decades thereafter. This is not the place for a deep dive on that, but it must be noted that the cultural policies of successive PRI governments closely mirrored those in other Latin American countries throughout the twentieth century. Virtually everywhere except Cuba, right or center-right governments suppressed communist art and boosted that of their own ideological camps.

Looming behind these actions was, and is, the power of the United States. In many cases, the United States installed these Latin American governments. In all cases, it was made it clear to the entire region: certain things simply would not be tolerated. Those things included communist art, of which Stridentism was a very early exemplar. As such, for Maples to have a career in the PRI-controlled diplomatic service, renouncing the politics of Stridentism was quite literally the cost of entry. He paid that cost, lived very comfortably, saw the world, and lived long enough to have everyone address him as *maestro*. Most of his comrades spent decades working in anonymous poverty because they would not pay. This pattern was repeated throughout the region. Presumably it was seen as very successful, since such policies, official and otherwise, remain in place. Diplomatic or academic posts are often the carrot, while the stick is everything from a blacklist to a shallow grave.

The number of communist writers who managed to survive, let alone thrive, is low, though of course they were never wiped out altogether. Those who had real success can be counted on one hand. The role of the US literary establishment in all this can be most clearly seen in these rare cases because, outside of these exceptions, that literary establishment played no role at all. It did nothing to bring any of this suppressed work to US readers, enforcing what amounted to an undeclared cultural embargo. But even when someone did manage to break through this embargo, yankee publishers and critics always managed to find a way to leave their communism behind.

This is how Pablo Neruda, a very public communist for approximately forty of his sixty-nine years of residence on earth, became best known here for a book of love poems written years before he joined the Party. It's how Gabriel García Marquez, an intimate friend of Fidel Castro for decades and a very radical journalist, was magically transformed into a cute old man full of fanciful folklore. And it's how Julio Cortázar hopscotched his way to being a player of postmodern games, rather than the committed anti-imperialist—very much in the Leninist sense of the term—that he was in real life.

What we are discussing here is the systematic erasure of communist literature, both from Latin America itself and in the yankee imagination of the region. This was such a success that, when Bolaño's work began to appear here, the writers I was around assumed that the poets and movements it mentioned were fictional. There were so many of them, after all, and none of us had ever heard of any of them. Surely, this was just world building? Because I had long been, as I remain, a full-time cook, I'd picked up enough Spanish to actually investigate the matter and found that no, they were not fictional. Having been a communist since I was a teenager, I was thrilled. Though I was not terribly literate in Spanish at this time, it having been primarily a language I spoke at work, I jumped in translating what I could, picking up literacy as I went. Eventually I sort of got the hang of it, and from then on I was all in.

I was, at one time, heavily involved in literary translation, editing a couple of journals, sitting on the panel for a translation award, publishing my own translations and so on. That, however, was more than a decade ago, and this is my first publication since. This is because by a certain point circa 2011, it became clear that the situation for communist literature in/from Latin America was no better than it had been on the iciest day of the Cold War. Literary readers in the United States, mostly good liberals then as now, remain as deeply and as silently committed to the yankee imperialism that makes them comfortable as they ever were. And just as fundamentally uninterested in anything coming from outside that consensus. I have not changed my mind on this question whatsoever. I was persuaded to return to the task, doing so mostly out of political commitment.

In a recent essay, Eugene Ostashevsky made the entirely correct observation that there "is no decolonization in English only." While I echo his demand that every

US reader learn more languages, I must also add: there is no decolonization without a confrontation with imperialism. Frantz Fanon is a better guide to the implications of that than I will ever be. But a real engagement with the cultures under the imperialist gun, rather than the usual passive consumption of literary commodities like this book, is one place we might start.

    — *KM Cascia*

The text of *Stridentist Poems* is set in Caslon Ionic, designed by Paul Barnes and Greg Gazdowicz for Commercial Classics in 2019, based on William Caslon's Ionic No. 2—a nineteenth-century Clarendon from which many twentieth-century newspaper typefaces were derived. Mexican typesetting in the early twentieth century was often limited to external supply, and classics like Caslon were often in use.

The cover image and frontispiece, designed by Andrew Bourne, are reconstructions of Fermín Revueltas' designs for the Stridentist journal *Irradiador*: an advertisement for El Buen Tono cigarettes and a woodcut of the avant-garde city. Typesetting by Don't Look Now. Printed and bound by KOPA in Lithuania.

WORLD POETRY

Jean-Paul Auxeméry
Selected Poems
tr. Nathaniel Tarn

Maria Borio
Transparencies
tr. Danielle Pieratti

Jeannette L. Clariond
Goddesses of Water
tr. Samantha Schnee

Jacques Darras
John Scotus Eriugena at Laon
tr. Richard Sieburth

Olivia Elias
Chaos, Crossing
tr. Kareem James Abu-Zeid

Phoebe Giannisi
Homerica
tr. Brian Sneeden

Zuzanna Ginczanka
Conscious Wild: Selected Poems
tr. Alex Braslavsky

Nakedness Is My End:
Poems from the Greek Anthology
tr. Edmund Keeley

Jazra Khaleed
The Light That Burns Us
ed. Karen Van Dyck

Jerzy Ficowski
Everything I Don't Know
tr. Jennifer Grotz & Piotr Sommer
PEN AWARD FOR POETRY IN TRANSLATION

Antonio Gamoneda
Book of the Cold
tr. Katherine M. Hedeen &
Víctor Rodríguez Núñez

Maria Laina
Hers
tr. Karen Van Dyck

Maria Laina
Rose Fear
tr. Sarah McCann

Perrin Langda
A Few Microseconds on Earth
tr. Pauline Levy Valensi

Manuel Maples Arce
Stridentist Poems
tr. KM Cascia

Enio Moltedo
Night
tr. Marguerite Feitlowitz

Meret Oppenheim
The Loveliest Vowel Empties:
Collected Poems
tr. Kathleen Heil

Elisabeth Rynell
Night Talks
tr. Rika Lesser

Giovanni Pascoli
Last Dream
tr. Geoffrey Brock
RAIZISS/DE PALCHI TRANSLATION AWARD

Rainer Maria Rilke
Where the Paths Do Not Go
tr. Burton Pike

Ardengo Soffici
Simultaneities & Lyric Chemisms
tr. Olivia E. Sears

Ye Lijun
My Mountain Country
tr. Fiona Sze-Lorrain

Verónica Zondek
Cold Fire
tr. Katherine Silver